Christianity UNRAVELED

Christianity
UNRAVELED

Unpacking the essentials of salvation

Jennifer Chamberlain

Christianity Unraveled

Published by
Inscript Publishing
a division of Dove Christian Publishers
P.O. Box 611
Bladensburg, MD 20710-0611
www.inscriptpublishing.com

Copyright © 2021 by Jennifer Chamberlain

Cover Design by Mark Yearnings

All rights reserved. No part of this publication may be used or reproduced without permission of the publisher, except for brief quotes for scholarly use, reviews or articles.

Scripture quotations, unless otherwise noted, are from the ESV® Bible (The Holy Bible, English Standard Version®), Copyright © 2001 by Crossway, a publishing ministry of Good News Publishers. Used by permission. All rights reserved.

Scriptures marked (KJV) are taken from the King James Version of the Bible. Public Domain.

ISBN: 978-1-7375177-2-6

Printed in the United States of America

Dedicated to my husband Pastor John Chamberlain.
I pray that our journey in ministry together continues
for a long time.

CONTENTS

Preface	1
What Christianity Has Become	5
The Complexity of the Church Today	10
The Earliest Believers	15
God is Real	23
The Virgin Birth	26
Christ Died for Our Sins	29
We Must Repent	32
The Resurrection	37
If You Don't Believe Me, Believe Paul	42
Living for Christ	46
Maturity	53
God's Word Brings Unity, Not Division	58
Tithing	71
Water Baptism	77
The Holy Spirit	81
Discerning Truth	89
Our Ideas	97
Conclusion	100

PREFACE

Take my yoke upon you, and learn from me, for I am gentle and lowly in heart, and you will find rest for your souls. For my yoke is easy, and my burden is light. (Matt. 11:28-30)

Have you ever felt that Christianity, salvation, was complicated? Differences of opinion in the church often get in the way of the simple truth of Christ's death and resurrection for our sins, and salvation becomes wound up with all kinds of other issues.

Repentance and a relationship with God take a back seat to topics that cause debate among the members of God's body, the church. Non-believers get confused, and new believers may leave the church, not knowing if the grace of God saves them. We cannot allow this to happen.

Christ said we are to find rest for our souls when we come to God. Our relationship with our Father should be easy and refreshing. He offers us peace and joy and all the fruit of the Holy Spirit. The church needs to take to heart what Paul said to Timothy.

O Timothy, guard the deposit entrusted to you. Avoid the irreverent babble and contradictions of what is falsely called "knowledge." (1 Timothy 6:20)

Unfortunately, we often do not rest in the knowledge

that Jesus Christ has saved us and that God will help us understand His word and how we should live. Instead, we argue and discuss topics that take our focus off Christ crucified and resurrected. We fashion a heavy yoke of rules, titles, and requirements and hang it gladly around our necks. We think Christianity must be difficult for us to be worthy.

Humankind has a great need to control what we do not always understand by naming them and adding a few rules just for good measure. We do not need words, works, or debate; we need a relationship with Christ.

Examples of terms that have made Christianity confusing to some are 'denomination', 'non-denominational', 'Pentecostal', 'charismatic', 'protestant', 'Catholic', 'nominal', 'spirit-filled, and more. Over time, these labels have developed as we strive to make our personal mark on what God gave us.

Along with these terms, we have added burdens to what Christ told us were supposed to be light burdens. We concern ourselves with rules and regulations that we believe might be in the Bible. We have complicated, twisted, studied, discussed, argued about, and even died for what Christ wanted us to enjoy.

We memorize scripture verses that are educational and uplifting, which is wonderful. I have listed several in this book as examples of various points. However, God's word can be made burdensome by taking scripture verses out of context and basing theology on just one verse or section.

Context tells us who wrote the scripture, to whom they were writing, and what was going on in the area or church at the time. It is valuable to carefully examine what we read and hear so that we do not add weighty unnecessary concerns that hurt our relationship with Christ.

Christianity is not burdensome. Christ told us this

truth. Let's unravel the foundation of Christ's teaching, and in doing so, toss away any burdens we are carrying.

Join me as I do my best, with God's guidance, to unravel some topics that can be confusing. I can't cover them all, but I will cover the most common ones that have been brought to my attention over the years.

When we allow ourselves to get caught up in issues and topics that have nothing to do with our salvation through Christ, we cause Christians, at whatever level of their relationship with God, to question their faith. It is a tactic of the devil to draw us away from the simple truth.

A story from my past:

Not long ago, in a retail store, I saw seven college-age students with clipboards trying to engage people in conversation. One of them approached me and asked if I knew that God is a woman. I tried my best to explain that there is neither male nor female in heaven, but he was in some 'Bible' college (a name I did not recognize) and, as college students often do, felt he knew more than I.

How many people were deceived that evening is unknown to me, but my heart was breaking. And why? What difference did it make? Even if (though the Bible is clear there is no male or female in heaven) God is a man, or if God is a woman, it has no bearing on our salvation. Why do we allow ourselves to get wrapped up in these types of worthless, time-wasting discussions?

What are we doing in the name of Christianity? Our salvation through Christ is a gift of grace, and we just keep meddling and twisting and leading others astray with our presumed knowledge.

When we begin to study scripture or other human ideologies pertaining to Christianity, we must always return to the basic message of Christ and the simple Christianity that He intended for us. Salvation is salvation through the grace (unmerited favor) of Christ.

In these last days, we will find more of this type of false teaching. Some will fall away from Christ because of the false teaching, burdens, and fears.

> **Now the Spirit expressly says that in later times some will depart from the faith by devoting themselves to deceitful spirits and teachings of demons, through the insincerity of liars whose consciences are seared, who forbid marriage and require abstinence from foods that God created to be received with thanksgiving by those who believe and know the truth. (1 Timothy 4:1-3)**

Christianity Unraveled examines what salvation through Christ requires and looks at scriptures that teach and guide us. The Bible is the Holy Spirit-inspired word of God given to us as historical information and instruction in living a Christ-like life and how we can obtain salvation through God's Son, Jesus. The Bible is to encourage, uplift, and make our lives better, not harder.

1

WHAT CHRISTIANITY HAS BECOME

*I*t is mind-boggling what Christianity has become in our churches today, with rituals and memorized sayings, bowing, robes, oil, and such. What is necessary to be a Christian seems complicated. The rules, suggestions, warnings, and regulations humans require to be 'religious' confuse us, especially if we lack wisdom in the things of the Lord.

According to the Center for the Study of Global Christianity, there were 5,500,000 congregations and 45,000 denominations in the world in 2019.[1]

Many churches say they are following Christ and teaching God's word, but like the 'Bible' college student telling me that God is a woman, there is much false teaching done in the name of Christ.

Churches and denominations have their own terminology and ways of acting, dressing, and living a particular lifestyle. These traditions come about over time. Those who practice these traditions can knowingly or unknowingly put pressure on attendees with expectations that have nothing to do with salvation through Christ.

---

1   Status of Global Christianity, 2019, in the Context of 1900–2050, The Center for the Study of Global Christianity, www.globalchristianity.org

There is a group (church) of followers of Christ who do not allow the women to cut their hair or wear pants, jewelry, or makeup. They do not allow television in their homes. They meet in homes and send out teachers by twos to travel and preach.

I admire things about this group, especially their dedication to God's Word and their support of each other. Their Bible teaching is primarily sound, but they feel that salvation is only possible (not assured) through living their lifestyle.

If this is what makes you comfortable, then attend this group. However, you must be aware that this lifestyle and these human rules are not Christ's rules, and they **do not, cannot, and will not** save you. Salvation comes through the grace of Christ.

Church fellowship members sometimes forget that self-righteousness can be a sin. Many churches believe that their way is the only way to heaven and that those who do not live their lifestyle have missed the mark. God sees our hearts, our love for Him, and our genuine repentance.

In the time of Paul, the area of Galatia had a situation that caused problems with the new believers. In Paul's letter to the Galatians, he is astonished that they are quickly deserting the uncomplicated faith they had learned from him and are turning to a different gospel by adding the unnecessary burden of circumcision.

Jewish Christians were telling the Gentile Christians that they must be circumcised. Even though the Galatians knew that Paul had not taught this, they were concerned that it might be true, causing confusion and division among the believers.

Some denominations and individual Christians try to add burdens just as the Jewish Christians did to the Gentile Galatians. With the number of denominations we now have, you can see why this might become a problem.

It reminds me of the story of the young, newly married woman who was cooking a roast. She cut off both ends before placing the roast in the roasting pan. Her husband asked her why she did this, and she said, "that's how my mother did it." Later she asked her mother why she cut both ends off the roast before cooking it, and her mother said, "That's how your grandma did it." So, they went to grandma and asked her the question. She answered, "Well, my pan was too small." Over time and losing the original meaning, may be how things in the church become fixed rules. Someone in the past had a too-small pan, and ever since, people have cut the ends off the roast.

> **I am astonished that you are so quickly deserting him who called you in the grace of Christ and are turning to a different gospel— not that there is another one, but there are some who trouble you and want to distort the gospel of Christ. But even if we or an angel from heaven should preach to you a gospel contrary to the one we preached to you, let him be accursed. As we have said before, so now I say again: If anyone is preaching to you a gospel contrary to the one you received, let him be accursed. (Galatians 1:2-9)**

> **Look: I, Paul, say to you that if you accept circumcision, Christ will be of no advantage to you. I testify again to every man who accepts circumcision that he is obligated to keep the whole law. You are severed from Christ, you who would be justified by the law; you have fallen away from grace. For through the Spirit, by faith, we ourselves eagerly wait for the hope of righteousness. For in Christ Jesus neither circumcision nor uncircumcision counts for anything, but only faith working through love. You were running well. Who hindered you from**

obeying the truth? This persuasion is not from him who calls you. A little leaven leavens the whole lump. I have confidence in the Lord that you will take no other view, and the one who is troubling you will bear the penalty, whoever he is. (Galatians 5:1-10)

For over 2000 years, believers have developed different theologies and varying styles of worship. We think our church has all the answers and that our ways will make God's ways better, as if He needs our additional input. How arrogant we can be.

Our salvation through unmerited favor from Christ does not depend on rules created by man or on what the church has become today. We need to know the difference between what God requires for our salvation and what He does not.

We can choose how we want to worship. We can choose a service formal or informal, small or large, loud or quiet, a small Bible study or a zoom service. We have every type imaginable to choose from, but Glory to God, our salvation does not depend on the type of church service we attend. If we hear God's word about Christ's crucifixion, resurrection, and repentance of sin and have fellowship with other believers, that is all that matters. We must be good judges of the words we hear today.

Christianity today is far from what it was after Christ's death and resurrection. The earliest followers of Christ believed in God, His Son, and the Holy Spirit. The teaching they received was what Jesus had taught the disciples about forgiveness, faith, peace, and love. They believed He was the promised Messiah and wanted to learn and live as He lived. Everything they did was to bring about a greater understanding of God's word. They dedicated themselves to the apostle's teaching, fellowship, and prayer. They desired a personal relationship with the Father.

We can follow their example to understand better the truth of salvation and the difference between what God requires of us, what the apostles suggested for specific groups and times, and what is of man and not of God. Then we will feel the true freedom promised us, not the burdens from our multitude of churches or denominations.

So Jesus said to the Jews who had believed him, **"If you abide in my word, you are truly my disciples, and you will know the truth, and the truth will set you free." (John 8:31-32)**

2

THE COMPLEXITY OF THE CHURCH TODAY

*I*t is clear, just by looking at the churches in the world today, how much it has changed over the last 2000 years. It is challenging to imagine how we got to where we are from where the earliest believers began.

Many churches consider themselves to be 'Christian.' Some are called Protestant, Catholic, Mormon, Universalists, or many other names. Some do not follow God's word or, they may try to add to it. Some take away from or disregard certain books. Some do not follow Christ or believe He is God.

We must be careful to attend Bible-believing churches but not judge other individuals by the church they attend. God looks at the heart of each individual, and it is not for us to say whether someone has come to salvation by simply believing, repenting, and living for Christ.

Worship styles vary in churches today, from singing a hymn now and then throughout the service to singing several choruses in a row before a sermon. Many churches sing hymns with organ music, or singers stand in the front and perform or lead the congregation in contemporary Christian music. There are large and small 'worship teams' with many instruments. Some churches do not allow musical instruments at all.

In some churches, men and women sit on opposite

sides of the room. Some churches require the congregation to stand while singing. Some sit on pews, chairs, in rows, or a circle. Some clap to the music and worship God with raised hands. Some are quiet and bow or kneel reverently. There are churches with dancers who have ribbons and flashing colored lights above the altar.

Preaching styles vary, too. Some preachers read their sermons, and some preach from memory. Some even preach about science or good works. There are even feel-good messages about acceptance of worldly people (of all types of sin). There are dynamic speakers and boring speakers, those with much to say and those with little. Some teach about God clearly, and some do not preach from the Bible at all.

Communion is different everywhere. There are churches where the bread and wine (or grape juice) are passed around every week and churches where communion is served monthly. There are churches where the Lord's supper is administered every three months or not at all, and there are services where the juice or wine is in a chalice passed from person to person. Some communion is served in tiny pre-filled cups.

We do not sell our possessions and give to each other as we see need anymore, but most churches pass an offering plate, and some ask that people drop their donations into a box at the back of the church. We can pay our tithes and offerings online now, too. Some churches have a 50,000 dollar a month budget, and some need only a few hundred dollars.

Some have bulletins to supply information about the service and other events. There are Sunday School classes and children's church, adult studies, and multiple adult church services.

The list goes on: sprinkling 'Holy water', confession to a priest, worship of Mary, the mother of Jesus, services in Latin only, quiet churches, loud churches, churches where women are not allowed to wear make-up or pants, churches where women dress up and men wear suits. The craziness of our churches is out of control. But still, it is not the church we attend that saves us.

We do not dedicate ourselves to the apostle's teachings like the earliest believers. We do not devote ourselves to prayer and fellowship. To commit ourselves to these things in the lives we have today may seem an impossibility. The average family has 1.93 children these days, and both parents are working to make ends meet. Add to that the over-scheduling that is often done for the entire family, and we barely have time to breathe.

Parents and guardians enroll children in soccer, baseball, music lessons, dance, youth clubs, after-school activities, and church activities. Parents work all day, shop, cook, clean, take care of children and pets, go out with friends, take classes, help with homework, pay bills, and participate in church activities, sometimes every night of the week.

Fellowship on Sunday or Saturday is in church. We may go to classes, and then during the service, we sing, pray, give tithes to the Lord, and hear a message. Then, someone prays again, and we go home or out to eat.

We are lucky to say a prayer in the morning and before we sleep at night, and our prayers may be haphazard and short. We are not enjoying an abundant life as Christ would define it. We are not devoting ourselves to teaching, fellowship, and prayer as the early Christians did. This burden is heavy. It is no wonder we don't have peace, but this is not what Christ wants.

We may think that early Christians had it much easier than we do now. There was no technology, and they were free to plan their schedules. The issue is time, we say. We do not have any.

Were the early Christians so much different? Did they have more than 24 hours in a day? Christians always have worked to support themselves and their families. Early Christians had many children to take care of and homes to keep clean. They had meals to prepare and debts to pay.

Women bought and sold property, managed their households, washed the saints' feet, showed hospitality, cared for the afflicted, and devoted themselves to every good work.

> **...and having a reputation for good works: if she has brought up children, has shown hospitality, has washed the feet of the saints, has cared for the afflicted, and has devoted herself to every good work. (1 Timothy 5:10)**

> **She considers a field and buys it; with the fruit of her hands she plants a vineyard. (Proverbs 31:16)**

The apostle Paul made tents to support himself, and many fished, farmed, or worked in some other manner. The point is they worked, both men and women, and they worked hard. They raised children, probably more than many of us have today. They learned musical instruments like the lyre, the flute, and the drum, purchased food and materials, and built houses by hand. They made their clothing and carried water from the well. They planted and harvested crops and raised livestock. Yet, they managed to devote themselves to the apostle's teaching, prayer, fellowship, and the breaking of bread together.

Is the life we live today what Jesus meant when He said:

> **"Take my yoke upon you, and learn from me, for I am gentle and lowly in heart, and you will find rest for your souls. For my yoke is easy, and my burden is light" (Matt. 11:28-30)**

Are we finding rest for our souls? Is the Christian burden light? If it is not, then it is time to adjust our own lives. It is not up to us to change others; we can only change ourselves and remember the basis of salvation, what is essential to God, and what is not. Each must decide how to live their lives for Christ.

Where we worship and how we worship do not determine our salvation. We believe, we repent, and we live for Christ. The rest will make our lives better, or we will allow the world to crowd in and make our lives stressful and difficult. The church today will help, or it will hinder.

We can not let our lives and our church 'requirements' be so overwhelming that we miss the mark of true Christianity.

3

THE EARLIEST BELIEVERS

And they devoted themselves to the apostles' teaching and the fellowship, to the breaking of bread and the prayers. And awe came upon every soul, and many wonders and signs were being done through the apostles. And all who believed were together and had all things in common. And they were selling their possessions and belongings and distributing the proceeds to all, as any had need. And day by day, attending the temple together and breaking bread in their homes, they received their food with glad and generous hearts, praising God and having favor with all the people. And the Lord added to their number day by day those who were being saved. (Acts 2:43-47)

*I*n the book of Acts, we find the record of the Apostles and what they were doing. Still, in Chapter 2, verses 43-47, we see a beautiful description of the lives and behaviors of the early converts following those Apostles after the day of Pentecost when the Holy Spirit fell, and they all spoke with other tongues. Pentecost is where it all began.

These eleven (later twelve) disciples became apostles (teachers) of Jesus. They began teaching others all the Lord had instructed them about His life, death, and resurrection, and about His grace to those who believed. This fellowship of believers was the start that has spread to become what we call Christianity today. At that time, they were called followers, believers, or people of The Way.

An apostle is someone who studied under a teacher (in this case, Jesus) and is sent to deliver those teachings to others. The title 'Apostle' means a messenger or one who is sent. Today, we are all apostles of Christ's teaching. Still, in the first days following the death and resurrection of Jesus, the only apostles were the eleven disciples (less Judas) that Christ had personally chosen to sit at His feet and learn how to live as God intended.

The Lord had many disciples (followers) following Him and listening to His teachings. Still, not all were chosen as part of the twelve, and not all were sent by Christ to go into the world and teach others as apostles.

Then the eleven disciples went to Galilee, to the mountain to which Jesus had directed them. And when they saw him, they worshiped him; but some doubted. And Jesus came and said to them, "All authority in heaven and on earth has been given to me. Go Therefore and make disciples of all nations, baptizing them in the name of the Father and of the Son and of the Holy Spirit, teaching them to observe all that I have commanded you. And behold, I am with you always, to the end of the age."(Matthew 28:16-20)

The early believer's devotion to fellowship and friendship listed in Acts 2:43-47 was significant because there were so few of them in any area. Like us, it is always comforting to associate with people who believe the same and act the same way. It is uncomfortable to be the only one who is different, so their bond was intense, especially when they were persecuted and hated for their faith.

From Strong's Exhaustive Concordance, we find that 'fellowship' is from koinonos; (Koinonia) meaning partnership, i.e. (literally) participation, or (social) intercourse, or (pecuniary) benefaction -- (to) communicate, communion, (contribution) distribution, fellowship.

Wikipedia.org says, "the essential meaning of the Koinonia embraces concepts conveyed in the English terms' community, communion, joint participation, sharing, and intimacy." The New American Standard Bible translates *koinonia* as fellowship twelve times, as sharing three times, and as participation and contribution twice each.

The followers of Christ who were under the tutelage of the disciples/apostles were joint participants who benefited from their community or fellowship. They were the first body of believers in partnership with one another. They were a family, not just people who gathered once a week. This fellowship is what Christ wanted then and what He wants now.

That they may all be one, just as you, Father, are in me, and I in you, that they also may be in us, so that the world may believe that you have sent me. The glory that you have given me I have given to them, that they may be one even as we are one, I in them and you in me, that they may become perfectly one, so that the world may know that you sent me and loved them even as you loved me. (John 17:21-23)

True fellowship within the body of Christ is a behavior we have moved away from as we all work our jobs and raise our families. We associate with unbelievers and are often not of the same mind as other Christians. Within our fellowship, we have rivalry, jealousy, and conceit. We think of ourselves first, and we look to our own interests. We add burdens to ourselves and each other under the guise of being better Christians.

We seclude ourselves because we are too lazy or tired from life to fellowship. We do not feel good enough, have nice enough clothes, give enough money, or attend every Sunday School class and Bible study. We may even believe we are harshly judged, or we may have been ignored when we last participated in a meeting.

Human nature and the evil of this world have drawn us away from true fellowship as experienced by the early believers. In these end times, the importance of connection will increase, and those who do not spend time with other Christians and gain strength from their encouragement and prayers may fall away, as Christ has warned.

Now the Spirit expressly says that in later times some will depart from the faith by devoting themselves to deceitful spirits and teachings of demons. (1 Timothy 4:1)

The early believers did not make a ceremony of each meal, but I am sure they remembered the Lord's sacrifice and the last supper as they broke bread together. Perhaps when Pentecost came each year, they more formally celebrated the Lord's body and blood, but that is not known and is one of those questions that is not worth debating.

The cup of blessing that we bless, is it not a participation in the blood of Christ? The bread that we break, is it not a participation in the body of Christ? Because there is one bread, we who are many are one body, for we all partake of the one bread. (1 Corinthians 10:16-17)

They received their food with glad hearts, and they were generous with each other.

And day by day, attending the temple together and breaking bread in their homes, they received their food with glad and generous hearts. (Acts 2:46)

We do not know if they ate every meal together, but just because Acts 20:7 speaks of them breaking bread on the first day of the week does not mean that is the only day they met together either. It would not surprise me to learn, when I get to Heaven, that many met together every day.

Remember that these new believers were a social community surrounded by non-believers just as we are today. Unfortunately, we sometimes hide our membership in our Christian society to not feel like outsiders in the world. If the early followers of Christ hid their beliefs, it was to avoid persecution and death. We are only fearful of not being accepted by the world, the world we are not supposed to be a part of anyway.

The new believers also devoted themselves to prayer. Some today also pray or talk to God constantly, but some seldom pray at all. And the way to pray that Christ taught His disciples has, to some, become a memorized ritual void of meaning.

Being devoted to prayer, or conversation with our Heavenly Father, is a privilege that the early believers understood. They could go directly to the source of their salvation. They had prayers they had memorized in the temple, but learning to pray from the Apostles in the way Christ taught was a very new experience.

We can only imagine what it must have been like sitting at the Apostles' feet and hearing the stories of Jesus and how they related to the Old Testament scriptures and the prophesies. There is nothing that could compare to knowing that they were the generation experiencing the fulfillment of the promises of God.

It is no wonder that they were so devoted to the apostle's teaching. The Adam Clark Commentary puts it this way. "They continued steadfastly in the apostles' doctrine - *They received it, retained it, and acted on its principles.*"

They received what they heard, and they remembered it, going on with their daily lives and acting on the principles taught to them. They wanted to learn about Christ and how He instructed them to live following their redemption from sins. So, they listened, worked at understanding, and put it to memory to use in their own lives.

People during that time often traveled or moved their families to other locations. They visited family members in other towns and told what they had been hearing. The apostles wrote letters, and when Paul became an apostle, he did not stay in one place, unless he was in prison, and wrote letters, keeping track of and teaching the people. Teachers of the gospel of Christ began traveling from area to area, and the good news spread. Other groups sprung up; many named after locations like the Corinthians from Corinth or the Thessalonians from Thessalonica.

Some studied to make sure the information taught lined up with the scriptures they knew.

Now these Jews were more noble than those in Thessalonica; they received the word with all eagerness, examining the Scriptures daily to see if these things were so. (Acts 17:11)

Day by day, they listened, studied, and applied what they learned to their lives to have great favor with all the people. Every day, they were together in the temple and then with the disciples. How joyous and simple these early gatherings must have been.

I am sure there was discussion, questions, and arguments until the apostles gave them direction. They were the experts because they had sat at the Lord's feet while He taught. There were no denominational separations, no dress code, and no worship team. They took no offering because they helped each other as they needed. Children sat with their parents and heard about Christ from their youth. The Holy Spirit performed miracles through the apostles and teachers.

These meetings were quite different than the formality of the Temple with which the Jews were familiar. The freedom must have felt incredible. Learning about mercy and grace and the gift of salvation would have been such a fantastic experience that must have made them want to run out and tell the world.

Proclaiming the kingdom of God and teaching about the Lord Jesus Christ with all boldness and without hindrance. (Acts 28:31)

And when he had found him, he brought him to Antioch. For a whole year they met with the church and taught a great many people. And in Antioch the disciples were first called Christians. (Acts 11:26)

They gathered for fellowship and to learn. They shared and helped those who were struggling. They rejoiced with those who were joyous, prayed for those in need, and cried with those who were mourning.

And let us consider how to stir up one another to love and good works, not neglecting to meet together, as is the habit of some, but encouraging one another, and all the more as you see the Day drawing near. (Hebrews 10:24-25)

Now the full number of those who believed were of one heart and soul, and no one said that any of the things that belonged to him was his own, but they had everything in common. (Acts 4:32)

Prayer was a significant part of their dedication. Picture those new Christians having just received shocking news: the Messiah had died for their sins and risen from the dead, that grace now abounded instead of the law. Their prayers were undoubtedly filled with thanksgiving, praise, and asking for others to come into the fold. They would have prayed for safety from the persecution that was happening and those imprisoned for their faith.

Some would have prayed for boldness, that they might stand firm in the face of danger, and I am sure they prayed for the wellbeing of their families. They prayed as Christ taught the disciples to pray in what we call the Lord's Prayer, beginning with praise and glorifying God, asking for more of His kingdom, and that they would know His will.

They prayed for their daily bread, not bread for the month or year but just enough to meet the needs of their families. They prayed for forgiveness and that they would forgive others. They prayed for guidance and deliverance. And they ended with more praise and thanksgiving.

The church as we know it has changed drastically from that of the earliest believers. We have not continued with faith, fellowship, prayer, and teaching. These were the keys to their lives and survival. Our behavior has changed to such an extent that Christianity is no longer straightforward. Christianity is not tricky. It has never been difficult. In these last days, while the world is falling apart, it is time for us to snap out of our self-focused ways and spread the Word of God, the Grace of God, and the Love of God to everyone we meet.

We can worship, fellowship, pray, and listen to teaching in any Bible-believing church, with any Bible-believing group, or alone. But when salvation or living a Christian life becomes a burden, we should be aware that there is a problem. We must return to the basics that we know are true, and then we will be in unity with all. And what are those fundamental beliefs that we need for salvation?

4

GOD IS REAL

1. Believe in God

For by grace you have been saved through faith. And this is not your own doing; it is the gift of God, (Ephesians 2:8)

The simplicity of Christianity is that salvation comes from faith in Christ, so to call ourselves Christians truly, there are truths that we must believe and accept in our hearts. These beliefs all work together to build our relationship with God, the Father.

The first, most obvious truth is that God is real and that He created the universe and the earth where we live. It would be difficult to believe in Jesus Christ, His son, without acknowledging that God is real. If there were no God, there would be no Son and no salvation.

In the beginning, God created the heavens and the earth. The earth was without form and void, and darkness was over the face of the deep. And the Spirit of God was hovering over the face of the waters. And God said, "Let there be light," and there was light. And God saw that the light was good. And God separated the light from the darkness. God called the light Day, and the darkness he called Night. And there was evening and there was morning, the first day... (Genesis 1:1-31)

The Word of God, the Bible, is clear about who God is and that the Spirit of God created the universe. There are many scriptures in the Bible about our Creator God and how He created the world.

"I am the Alpha and the Omega," says the Lord God, "who is and who was and who is to come, the Almighty." (Revelation 1:8)

God was in the beginning and will be forever. He is outside of time and space, as we understand it. God is and was and is to come. He is forever, past, present, and future. He is the great 'I Am.' **He is spirit.**

God is spirit, and those who worship him must worship in spirit and truth." (John 4:24)

Just as we know that God is spirit, we also know that matter makes up everything in the universe. I am no scientist or theologian, but I do know that books and chairs do not fall from the sky fully formed. Everything in the universe is made by someone or comes from something (matter) that was made. Even those who believe in the big bang theory must agree that the big bang did not happen out of nothing. Everything comes from matter that had to have been created by someone.

If everything that exists comes out of something and is created by someone, then there must be a creator, and that creator must be spirit, not of matter, and have existed eternally. Otherwise, the creator would also have had to be created by someone else.

For by him all things were created, in heaven and on earth, visible and invisible, whether thrones or dominions or rulers or authorities—all things were created through him and for him. (Colossians 1:16)

Webster's dictionary defines God as the creator and ruler of the universe and source of all moral authority; the supreme being, a superhuman being or <u>spirit</u> worshiped as having power over nature or human fortunes; a deity.

Having a Spirit Creator is far beyond our human comprehension. Still, since we know that everything was created out of something and by someone, we can reason that the universe was created by a supreme being who has always existed in spirit, who was and is and is to come. We call that creator God.

I am always surprised to find those who believe in spirits and talking to the dead deny that there could be a God, Spirit, and loving Creator/Father.

For thus says the Lord, who created the heavens (he is God!), who formed the earth and made it (he established it; he did not create it empty, he formed it to be inhabited!): 'I am the Lord, and there is no other.' (Isaiah 45:18)

God is real, and He created the universe and the earth we inhabit. Does this mean that God did not make anything else or any other place, planet, or people? We do not know the answer to that question, and we do not need to know. Belief in a creator God is a simple truth required of us for salvation through Christ, His Son.

If others tell us we must believe that God did not create any other place, or if they tell us that He did and that we must believe it to be Christian, this is additional and unnecessary. Thinking one way or another about this subject has nothing to do with our salvation through Christ. We do not have to understand everything.

To have a relationship with someone, we must believe that they exist. Therefore, Christians believe in one God, the creator, and that He is the only God that exists.

There is one body and one Spirit—just as you were called to the one hope that belongs to your call— one Lord, one faith, one baptism, one God and Father of all, who is over all and through all and in all. (Ephesians 4:5b-6)

5

THE VIRGIN BIRTH

1. **Believe in God**
2. **Believe in the Virgin Birth of Christ**

We also must believe that Jesus, the bodily form of God, was sent by God and was born of a virgin. His miraculous birth shows the world that He was not just a man. He was conceived of the Holy Spirit and was fully man and fully God. The virgin birth prophesied hundreds of years prior occurred, and many historical records support Christ's birth, birthplace, life, and death.

> *Regarding the Old Testament, it is perhaps the most accurately reproduced ancient text in the entire world. Scribes took great care because they were writing God's word. We know the accuracy of the text has been beyond reproach for at least 2,500 years. The discovery of the Dead Sea scrolls confirms this.*
>
> *Regarding the New Testament, we possess enough of the writings of early church leaders who wrote within about 100 years of Christ's resurrection to be able to reproduce the gospels and letters of Paul and John. There are over 20,000 handwritten manuscripts of the New Testament from the first few centuries of Christianity, written in Coptic, Greek, Latin, Syriac, and other languages. There are 5,700 New Testament Greek manuscripts known to exist,*

and some of those were written within about 100 years of Christ's resurrection.[2]

Therefore the Lord himself will give you a sign. Behold, the virgin shall conceive and bear a son, and shall call his name Immanuel. (Isaiah 7:14 Old Testament)

In the book of Isaiah, when God spoke to the prophet Ahaz, God promised that a virgin would conceive and bear a son. Isaiah lived approximately 700 years before Christ was born. The Jewish people waited for this promise and recorded it when it happened.

Now the birth of Jesus Christ took place in this way. When his mother Mary had been betrothed to Joseph, before they came together, she was found to be with child from the Holy Spirit. And her husband Joseph, being a just man and unwilling to put her to shame, resolved to divorce her quietly. But as he considered these things, behold, an angel of the Lord appeared to him in a dream, saying, "Joseph, son of David, do not fear to take Mary as your wife, for that which is conceived in her is from the Holy Spirit. She will bear a son, and you shall call his name Jesus, for he will save his people from their sins." All this took place to fulfill what the Lord had spoken by the prophet: ... (Matthew 1:18-22)

The virgin birth was all part of God's plan to bring us back into the close, trusting relationship with Him that we lost when Adam and Eve brought sin into the world.

Before Christ was born of the virgin, whose name was Mary, and before His gift of salvation through grace, a

---

[2] Erickson, Erick. "The Authenticity of the Virgin Birth, by Erick Erickson." , By Erick Erickson | Creators Syndicate, 25 Dec. 2020, www.creators.com/read/erick-erickson/12/20/the-authenticity-of-the-virgin-birth-60f06.

law was given to Moses for the people to follow. The law was only a temporary fix for the people's relationship with God. Humankind was not ready to understand grace yet. In this law, blood sacrifices were made for the people's sins and symbolized the coming blood sacrifice of Christ on the cross.

The virgin birth of the perfect Christ was the beginning of the permanent fix and fulfilled prophecies taught to the Israelites since childhood. The virgin birth of Christ is a simple truth we can believe because we can read the prophecies in the Old Testament and see how God worked in the hearts of the people to prepare them for this new covenant of grace.

God's Son, Jesus Christ, was sent to save us from our sins, and knowing that He was both God, Spirit, <u>and man </u>is vital to our relationship with God and our salvation through Him.

And the Word became flesh and dwelt among us, and we have seen his glory, glory as of the only Son from the Father, full of grace and truth. (John 1:14)

When it was time for God to bring His plan to fruition and fulfill the Old Testament's prophecies, He sent His son, Jesus, to be born of a virgin, grow, preach, heal, perform miracles, and die on the cross for our sins.

God, who we know is Spirit, virtually sent Himself (His Spirit) in bodily form, with a soul just like us. Jesus was entirely man and God, and though there is no male or female in heaven, He came as a male to the earth because only males had the power to command attention in that age.

6

CHRIST DIED FOR OUR SINS

1. **Believe in God**
2. **Believe in the Virgin Birth**
3. **Believe in Christ's death on the cross for our sins**

The people made blood sacrifices under the law given by God to Moses, and we know that this was only until the time was right for God to send His Son. Jesus became the final blood sacrifice for sin. We no longer must sacrifice the blood of lambs and goats for the forgiveness of sin. Christ died once for all.

> **For God so loved the world, that he gave his only Son, that whoever believes in him should not perish but have eternal life. (John 3:16)**
>
> **Indeed, under the law almost everything is purified with blood, and without the shedding of blood there is no forgiveness of sins. (Hebrews 9:22)**
>
> **For the life of the flesh is in the blood, and I have given it for you on the altar to make atonement for your souls, for it is the blood that makes atonement by the life. (Leviticus 17:11)**

Christ's death on the cross as a sacrifice for the sins of the world set us free from the law of Moses. The old covenant that God had made with the children of Israel ended, and the new covenant of grace through Christ began. It is belief and acceptance of Christ's death on the cross that is critical for our salvation.

> **He himself bore our sins in his body on the tree, that we might die to sin and live to righteousness. By his wounds you have been healed. (1 Peter 2:24)**

> **But God shows his love for us in that while we were still sinners, Christ died for us. (Romans 5:8)**

If Christ had not shed His blood for our sins, we would die as sinners, unworthy of eternity with our perfect God. Our sin would separate us from God forever. We believe and acknowledge that the blood of Christ cleanses us. We are not perfect, and we will never be perfect. Only Christ's blood allows us to come before our God sinless.

> **For Christ also suffered once for sins, the righteous for the unrighteous, that he might bring us to God, being put to death in the flesh but made alive in the spirit... (1 Peter 3:18)**

Christ's death was not just any death. He was beaten, tortured, nailed to a cross, and buried in a borrowed grave. He gave Himself freely to this. He had done nothing wrong. He had no sin but took the sins of the world, past, present, and future, upon Himself so that we could live. We need only trust and have faith in this freely given gift.

> **For the wages of sin is death, but the free gift of God is eternal life in Christ Jesus our Lord. (Romans 6:23)**

> **For by grace you have been saved through faith. And this is not your own doing; it is the gift of God, not a result of works, so that no one may boast. (Ephesians 2:8-9)**

We cannot earn our way to heaven. Salvation is freely given to us by God our Father. We cannot stand before God and say we helped others, fed the hungry, housed the homeless, clothed the naked, and expect to be welcomed into His presence. These are beautiful things to do, and God loves that we do them, but alone, they are worthless. Only faith in Christ and belief in His sacrifice on the cross will save us.

Not everyone who says to me, 'Lord, Lord,' will enter the kingdom of heaven, but the one who does the will of my Father who is in heaven. On that day many will say to me, 'Lord, Lord, did we not prophesy in your name, and cast out demons in your name, and do many mighty works in your name?' And then will I declare to them, 'I never knew you; depart from me, you workers of lawlessness.' (Matthew 7: 21-23)

7

WE MUST REPENT

1) **Believe in God**
2) **Believe in the Virgin Birth**
3) **Believe in Christ's death on the cross for our sins**
4) **Repent of our sins**

If we confess our sins, he is faithful and just to forgive us our sins and to cleanse us from all unrighteousness. (1 John 1:9)

When we accept that Christ died for the world's sins, we, individually, are sorry for and repent of our sins. Sometimes it is difficult to admit that we have done something that God considers a sin. Often, we think that a little white lie is not bad; we are not murderers, after all. The world has made a list of bad things that range, in our minds, from not so bad to horrible. This listing of sins is a worldly lie. Wrong is wrong, bad is bad, and sin is sin. And we have all sinned and will sin because we are not perfect.

We are constantly failing. All of us sin daily, even unknowingly. But staying in a close relationship with Christ, talking with Him regularly, and asking for His help and guidance, keeps us cleansed by His blood. Our hearts will be right with God because we know we are imperfect and must have the blood of Christ washing us daily. We must admit that we are sinners and confess our sins to God and ask for forgiveness. We can go directly to God and need not go through an intermediary.

What then? Are we Jews any better off? No, not at all. For we have already charged that all, both Jews and Greeks, are under sin, as it is written: "None is righteous, no, not one; (Romans 9:9-10)

Admitting that we are sinners and being contrite is how we show our faith in His death on the cross. Believing that Christ exists is not enough.

If we believe God sent His Son to be born of a virgin and die on the cross for our sins, we are doing well. But if we do not **repent** of our sins and ask for forgiveness, we make the gift worthless. We cannot live a sinful life and expect to spend eternity with God while only believing in Him and His sacrifice.

You believe that God is one; you do well. Even the demons believe—and shudder! (James 2:19)

The demons do not go to heaven even though they believe in God and His son. They do not repent of their sins, and they continue to do evil. Believing in something requires action. Knowing that there are viruses in our world today will not protect us from getting them. We must take action to protect ourselves and others. We must show our beliefs by our behavior.

We, then, must not only believe but repent of our sins, seeking forgiveness that Christ gives freely. We do not have to work for it. We do not have to wait until we are better people. Jesus loves and accepts us as we are. We have only to believe and repent.

But this is the covenant that I will make with the house of Israel after those days, declares the Lord: I will put my law within them, and I will write it on their hearts. And I will be their God, and they shall be my people. (Jeremiah 31:33)

God has written His will on our hearts just as He promised through Jeremiah. We know right from wrong. Sin may seem difficult to define, especially in today's world where anything we want to say or do is acceptable, but what sin is in God's eyes is not difficult to identify.

We know what is evil and displeasing to Him because His Holy Spirit tells us. In the world, the lines of what is sin and what is not are becoming blurred. Non-believers say that some actions or thoughts are not so bad or not sin at all, but in the eyes of God, there is no hierarchy of sin. Every sin is the same as any other. Murder is no worse than envy. Having sex before marriage is still a sin, even though the world says it is not. God does not change His mind.

Not only do we know what is right in our hearts, but God's word also lists most sins committed in the world. These sins are works of the flesh because they are not from God's Holy Spirit, and our flesh drives us to them. Our flesh can get us into a world of hurt and separate us from God for eternity.

Now the works of the flesh are evident: sexual immorality, impurity, sensuality, idolatry, sorcery, enmity, strife, jealousy, fits of anger, rivalries, dissensions, divisions, envy, drunkenness, orgies, and things like these. I warn you, as I warned you before, that those who do such things will not inherit the kingdom of God. (Galatians 5:19-21)

We do not get to choose what is and is not sin. Getting drunk is the same as fits of anger. These are the things we know are wrong and for which we should repent. We are born into sin. Even small children instinctively know right from wrong and, when asked, "Who broke the lamp?" will reply, "I don't know," even if they did it. We must ask God for forgiveness and avoid these sins and the people who practice them. We are not perfect, but God forgives a truly contrite heart. That is repentance.

Today the world is constantly moving forward to self-centered actions and greed. It is becoming acceptable to allow anyone to do anything they wish, but this is not the will of God.

Is God mean? Is He trying to spoil our fun? Not at all. He has told us what is wrong to keep us safe, healthy, and have the peace and joy we are desperately seeking. Look at sin and think about what it has caused in the world.

If we obeyed God, there would be less disease, road rage, shootings, anger, hatefulness, mental illness, deceit, and spite. Today, when these things happen, instead of blaming ourselves for what we have caused to happen in the world, we blame God. Taking responsibility for our sins, past, present, and future, and asking for His forgiveness, is the act of repentance vital for our salvation and sorely lacking in today's world.

For sin will have no dominion over you, since you are not under law but under grace. (Romans 6:14)

Evil, the enemy of God, yes, the devil, has convinced us that our temporary happiness is more important than anything else. It is all about us. Being 'happy' sounds like a perfectly logical goal, but God wants us to have 'joy' and 'peace' that are eternal and what we truly want. We do not get peace and joy from the world. They are given to us by the Holy Spirit.

We say we care about the planet and that all lives matter, but what it comes down to is our success, possessions, glory, entertainment, and self-satisfaction. If it feels good, it must be ok. But it is only with God that we will genuinely love our neighbor as much as we love ourselves and, in that way, have peace and unity. Salvation is not only easy; it is joyous. We must open our eyes, and yes, snap out of it.

For the kingdom of God is not a matter of eating and drinking but of righteousness and peace and joy in the Holy Spirit. (Romans 14:17)

When we accept the gift of Christ's death and repent of our sins, we are what Christ calls 'born again.' We are made new in Christ. When we ask for forgiveness of these sins, Christ's blood cleanses us and makes us new creations in Him. He writes His desires on our hearts so that instinctively we know what we should be choosing. Every decision we make is a 'fork in the road' moment in our lives. Will we go God's way or our own?

Therefore, if anyone is in Christ, he is a new creation. The old has passed away; behold, the new has come. (2 Corinthians 5:17)

"So whoever knows the right thing to do and fails to do it, for him it is sin." (James 4:17)

8

THE RESURRECTION

1) **Believe in God**
2) **Believe in the Virgin Birth**
3) **Believe in Christ's death on the cross for our sins**
4) **Repent of our sins**
5) **Believe in His resurrection from the dead**

Our eternity with God is assured with one final truth, that Christ rose from the dead and lives eternally with God, the Father. **When we believe in God, the virgin birth, Christ's death on the cross, and we ask for forgiveness of our sins and believe that He rose to life again, we have salvation through Christ.** We do not have to do anything else, wear any unique clothes, or change our basic personality. God created us the way we are for a reason.

His resurrection from the dead was to show us, again, that though He was fully man and His body died, He was also God in the flesh and could not die. He is eternal. He lives.

He has shown us that we will all live eternally with Him or without Him, depending on what we choose. Just as Christ lives eternally, we also do not die. The question we must answer is 'where do we want to spend eternity?' There are two choices according to God's word. We can spend eternity with God or apart from Him. One brings perfect joy, and the other brings dreadful pain and grief. We can freely choose eternal life or eternal misery. It is so simple. It is so easy, and yet we can make it so hard.

If the Spirit of him who raised Jesus from the dead dwells in you, he who raised Christ Jesus from the dead will also give life to your mortal bodies through his Spirit who dwells in you. (Romans 8:11)

Our Lord's body was taken down from the cross and placed in a borrowed grave. A large and heavy rock was placed before the opening. Old Testament prophets had proclaimed that the Messiah was to rise from the dead, so the leaders of the day placed several guards at the tomb to make sure the disciples didn't come and steal the body. They thought the disciples would lie, telling the people that He rose.

Some have argued that the doctrine of a bodily resurrection was unknown to the Israelites of the Old Testament. In fact, this denial was a cardinal doctrine of the sect of the Sadducees at the time of Christ.[3]

The same day Sadducees came to him, who say that there is no resurrection, and they asked him a question (Matthew 22:23)

Our text, however, makes it clear that this promise has always been known to the people of God. Long before Isaiah's time, Job had said: *"I know that my redeemer liveth, and that He shall stand at the latter day upon the earth; And... in my flesh shall I see God" (Job 19:25-26 KJV)*

After the time of Isaiah, the promise was still known.[4]

---

[3] Resurrection in the Old Testament, HENRY M. MORRIS, PH.D., Institution for Creation Research, https://www.icr.org/article/19662

[4] https://www.icr.org article, *Resurrection in the Old*

"Many of them that sleep in the dust of the earth shall awake, some to everlasting life, and some to shame and everlasting contempt" (Daniel 12:2).

The disciples were so lost when Christ died. They were in deep grief and were scattered and afraid that they might also be put to death because they were followers of Christ. They could not and did not steal Christ's body away in the night without the legion of guards noticing.

Christ rose from the dead after three days just as had been prophesied, and the guards were not even aware. Hundreds of people saw him after His resurrection. Jesus appeared to the disciples alone and then to many others.

Now after the Sabbath, toward the dawn of the first day of the week, Mary Magdalene and the other Mary went to see the tomb. And behold, there was a great earthquake, for an angel of the Lord descended from heaven and came and rolled back the stone and sat on it. His appearance was like lightning, and his clothing white as snow. And for fear of him the guards trembled and became like dead men. But the angel said to the women, "Do not be afraid, for I know that you seek Jesus who was crucified. ... (Matthew 28:1-5)

And he said to them, "Do not be alarmed. You seek Jesus of Nazareth, who was crucified. He has risen; he is not here. See the place where they laid him. (Mark 16:6)

For I delivered to you as of first importance what I also received: that Christ died for our sins in accordance with the Scriptures, that he was buried, that he was raised on the third day

---

Testament, The Institute for Creation Research

> in accordance with the Scriptures, and that he appeared to Cephas, then to the twelve. Then he appeared to more than five hundred brothers at one time, most of whom are still alive, though some have fallen asleep. Then he appeared to James, then to all the apostles. ... (1 Corinthians 15:3-7)

> Now when he rose early on the first day of the week, he appeared first to Mary Magdalene, from whom he had cast out seven demons. (Mark 16:9)

> On the evening of that day, the first day of the week, the doors being locked where the disciples were for fear of the Jews, Jesus came and stood among them and said to them, "Peace be with you." When he had said this, he showed them his hands and his side. Then the disciples were glad when they saw the Lord. Jesus said to them again, "Peace be with you. As the Father has sent me, even so I am sending you." And when he had said this, he breathed on them and said to them, "Receive the Holy Spirit. If you forgive the sins of any, they are forgiven them; if you withhold forgiveness from any, it is withheld." ... (John 20:19-23)

Following His resurrection and appearing to so many, He then ascended into heaven as they stood watching Him go.

> And when he had said these things, as they were looking on, he was lifted up, and a cloud took him out of their sight. And while they were gazing into heaven as he went, behold, two men stood by them in white robes, and said, "Men of Galilee, why do you stand looking into heaven? This Jesus, who was taken up from you into heaven, will come in the same way as you saw him go into heaven." (Acts 1:9-11)

Our Lord Jesus Christ will come again, and those of us **who believe in God, Christ's virgin birth, His life, death, and resurrection, will spend eternity with Him if we repent of our sins and accept His great gift.** Nothing should be added to or taken away from being born again through faith in Jesus Christ.

Discussions, arguments, and even church doctrine can draw us away from this simple salvation. Christ's burden is light. Remember to always come back to the simple truth - **<u>Believe, repent, and live for Him.</u>**

Blessed be the God and Father of our Lord Jesus Christ! According to His great mercy, he has caused us to be born again to a living hope through the resurrection of Jesus Christ from the dead. (1 Peter 1:3)

Because, if you confess with your mouth that Jesus is Lord and believe in your heart that God raised him from the dead, you will be saved. For with the heart one believes and is justified, and with the mouth one confesses and is saved. (Romans 10:9-10)

9

IF YOU DON'T BELIEVE ME, BELIEVE PAUL

Ephesians Chapters 2-4

And you were dead in the trespasses and sins in which you once walked, following the course of this world, following the prince of the power of the air, the spirit that is now at work in the sons of disobedience— among whom we all once lived in the passions of our flesh, carrying out the desires of the body and the mind, and were by nature children of wrath, like the rest of mankind. But God, being rich in mercy, because of the great love with which he loved us, even when we were dead in our trespasses, made us alive together with Christ— by grace you have been saved— (Ephesians 2:1-5)

Those who are wiser than I believe that Paul's letter to the Ephesians was called a circular letter, or one that was to be passed around to various churches so all could understand the basics of our salvation and the importance of unity in the body of Christ. The entire book is an essential source of information about God's plan for our relationship with Him and other believers.

He begins chapter 2 by saying that we are all sinners. We used to follow the world and Satan, the enemy of God. We are by nature sinners and were dead in our sins, but God, through Christ, has made us alive again. We are saved only by the grace of God. Grace is <u>unmerited</u> favor. We do not deserve it, but God gives it to us anyway.

For by grace you have been saved through faith. And this is not your own doing; it is the gift of God, not a result of works, so that no one may boast. For we are his workmanship, created in Christ Jesus for good works, which God prepared beforehand, that we should walk in them. (Ephesians 2: 8-10)

Ephesians chapter 2 **is** Christianity in its simplest form. We believe in Christ, and we are saved through our faith in Him by God's grace. We do not earn our way to heaven by doing good works, but God prepared good works ahead of time so that we could do them. We are by nature sinners and must repent, not following the world but living for Christ.

He speaks of two main groups at that time: the Jewish people who, under the law of Moses, were required to be circumcised, and the Gentiles, who were not circumcised and did not follow the law of Moses. These two groups of people did not get along. They did not work or talk with each other. Christ died for everyone; both the Gentiles and Jewish people were following Him and being baptized with both water baptism and the baptism of the Holy Spirit.

Circumcision was not required because it was an instruction given under the law of Moses. We do circumcise male babies today, primarily for health reasons, but these people were now under the promise of God, the new covenant through Christ Jesus, and the Gentiles didn't need to follow the old Jewish law. The Apostles had met to discuss this very issue and agreed that it was not necessary for the Gentiles. Everyone was and is welcome to come into a relationship with God. Followers of Christ were now all one body as we are today.

> **Therefore remember that at one time you Gentiles in the flesh, called "the uncircumcision" by what is called the circumcision** [Jewish people or the children of Israel], **which is made in the flesh by hands— remember that you were at that time separated from Christ, alienated from the commonwealth of Israel and strangers to the covenants of promise, having no hope and without God in the world. But now in Christ Jesus you who once were far off have been brought near by the blood of Christ. For he himself is our peace, who has made us both one and has broken down in his flesh the dividing wall of hostility by abolishing the law of commandments expressed in ordinances, that he might create in himself one new man in place of the two, so making peace (Ephesians 2:11-15)**

Paul was explaining that we are all one in Christ. There should be no hostility between people who believe in Christ. The law is gone. We all have direct access to the Father. We do not need to go through anyone else to talk to God or repent and be forgiven of our sins. God in Christ forgives us. We are loved beyond measure.

It is through faith in Christ and God's great love for us that we are saved. It is beyond our ability to understand God's love for us, but that is the simplicity of Christianity. Everything else is for teaching, reproof, correction, and training.

> **All Scripture is breathed out by God and profitable for teaching, for reproof, for correction, and for training in righteousness, (2 Timothy 3:16)**

In chapter 4, Paul sums up so beautifully what we can have in Christ, encouraging the believers to walk in unity, rooted and grounded in love, even while he was in prison in Rome.

For this reason I bow my knees before the Father, from whom every family in heaven and on earth is named, that according to the riches of his glory he may grant you to be strengthened with power through his Spirit in your inner being, so that Christ may dwell in your hearts through faith—that you, being rooted and grounded in love, may have strength to comprehend with all the saints what is the breadth and length and height and depth, and to know the love of Christ that surpasses knowledge, that you may be filled with all the fullness of God. (Ephesians 3:14-19)

Believe, repent, and live for Christ.

10

LIVING FOR CHRIST

Living for Christ is a choice we make when we believe in Him and repent of our sins. It is not always easy because worldly people who do not know Him will, at times, judge and ridicule those of us who do. This ridicule will happen more often as the day draws near for Christ's return.

We are human, and we can become angry and hurt or embarrassed because of our faith. We may want to lash out or become defensive. It can be challenging to behave as Christ would, and we will often fail because we are human and not perfect as He was. We can only do the best we can and lean on the Holy Spirit to help us know that when we fail, we are forgiven, sometimes not by man, but always by God.

For all have sinned and fall short of the glory of God. (Romans 3:23)

Because we love Him and know that He died for our sins, we can instead feel sympathy for non-believers who do not understand the peace and joy we have. With God's Holy Spirit living through us, strengthening us to respond with loving and kind actions, we can show who God is and what He offers to anyone who chooses Him.

You may have heard the saying, "Smile; they won't know what you are up to." Our motto should be "Smile; they will want to know what is up with you." Then we can tell what Christ has done for us. We are born again in Christ. We are made clean and new by our acceptance of Him. We get to start over. What could be better than that?

While working in an office with many non-believers, I often found myself smiling at jokes of which God would disapprove. When single, I even dated non-believers, but I found no joy in that lifestyle. God spoke clearly to me and drew me into an ever-closer relationship with Him until those things became so uncomfortable that I could not continue. Being pulled by both sides, the world and Christ, is not fun. We cannot ride the fence. Not making a clear decision for God is a decision against God.

Instead of trying to fit into the world, we can influence anyone we meet just by how we live our lives. Our actions as we live for Christ can make a difference in another person's life in our work, our homes, with extended family and friends. We may never see Christ's impact on them through us, but He is working to bring everyone into a relationship with Him. Christ calls us to help further His plan by our actions and reactions as we live for Him.

At times we may want to talk about God and tell others what He has done for us, especially when we first become new creations, but our actions speak loudly also. How we react to events around us or adversity in our own lives speaks volumes about our Christianity to others.

I have been crucified with Christ. It is no longer I who live, but Christ who lives in me. And the life I now live in the flesh I live by faith in the Son of God, who loved me and gave himself for me. (Galatians 2:20)

An offhand remark or responding in anger, even laughing at a bad joke, will inevitably bring about a comment: "I thought you were supposed to be a Christian."

Nothing cuts deeper into our hearts as that statement, but once we have acted or spoken in an un-Christ-like manner, it is too late to take it back. We can apologize. We can explain. But non-believers will remember our actions.

There are too many hypocritical Christians in the world today. At one time or another, we all are hypocrites. We may not intend to be, but our actions and attitude can destroy a person's faith, lead a young Christian into sin, or cause others to see Christianity as a big joke. Once born again, we represent Christ in everything we do and speak.

People should not judge Christianity by the behavior of Christ's followers, but they do. The world judges Christianity by the actions and attitudes of Christians. We should take care to show Christ's compassion, understanding, and love as best we can.

So put away all malice and all deceit and hypocrisy and envy and all slander. Like newborn infants, long for the pure spiritual milk, that by it you may grow up into salvation— if indeed you have tasted that the Lord is good. As you come to him, a living stone rejected by men but in the sight of God chosen and precious, you yourselves, like living stones are being built up as a spiritual house, to be a holy priesthood, to offer spiritual sacrifices acceptable to God through Jesus Christ. (1 Peter 2:1-5)

We know what sin is and that most are due to selfish, self-centered pride. We know right from wrong since God wrote His will on our hearts, but the world tells us something different. The world does not believe in sin and tries to convince us that there is no such thing. Unbelievers try to draw us into behavior that is not fitting for a follower of Christ. Then, when we join in their action, they ridicule and judge us. It is not fair, but Christianity is the truth, and the devil does not want the truth to be known.

Living in a world where it is ordinary for couples to live together without marriage, where drunkenness and parties are considered normal, and where we all have "rights" at the expense of others can tempt us to justify some of our actions. We know these actions do not please God, but we ignore Him and continue with our plans and living situations.

If our sins are holding us back from accepting the truth of Christ, we are truly lost. However, if we give ourselves wholeheartedly to God, He will bless us, and our lives will be so much better than they are when we are still sinning. It may seem difficult or nearly impossible, but whatever sinful situation you are in, get out of it now. God will bless you.

Christianity is simple, but so is sin. Hear this. The enemy of God has made sinning easy, accessible, and acceptable. We are more likely to be looked down upon and made fun of for following Christ than we are for sinning. That is why the world is in such a sad state.

I appeal to you therefore, brothers, by the mercies of God, to present your bodies as a living sacrifice, holy and acceptable to God, which is your spiritual worship. Do not be conformed to this world, but be transformed by the renewal of your mind, that by testing you may discern what is the will of God, what is good and acceptable and perfect. (Romans 12:1-2)

It used to be that most people in the United States, at least, were faithful Bible-believing Christians. That is not true now. Just because we live in a self-proclaimed Christian nation does not mean that people honestly believe in God, Christ, His virgin birth, death for our sins, and resurrection from the dead. And they most certainly do not believe in sin or make a choice to live for Him. They live for themselves alone.

Following Christ's death and resurrection, the Apostle's main job was to point out to the Israelites that Christ was the messiah foretold in what we call the Old Testament. They believed in God, that He existed, and had created the universe. Gentiles believed in a God, or one of many, so even they had a head start on the world today.

Finding someone now who knows without a doubt that there is a God can be a struggle. Many are agnostics (not knowing if there is a God or not) or atheists, who believe there is no God and that when we die, that is the end. There is nothing after death.

Is it any wonder that we have become so focused on ourselves and our enjoyment? If there is no God, there is no hell, no punishment, and life becomes a free-for-all. That is the world we are living in today.

To truly live for Christ among people with no beliefs and those who worship false gods can be grueling and exhausting, so we need to remember the basics of our salvation and not take on any added burdens. We need to snap out of complacency and disagreements among our Christian brothers and sisters.

Those who know the truth about the Christian life, what Christians experience, and what we will gain when our physical bodies give out seem like fools to those who don't believe. Even King David understood that there would always be those who do not understand and do not care about seeking to know God.

To the choirmaster. Of David. The fool says in his heart, "There is no God." They are corrupt, they do abominable deeds, there is none who does good. The LORD** looks down from heaven on the children of man, to see if there are any who understand, who seek after God. They have all turned aside; together they have become**

corrupt; there is none who does good, not even one. Have they no knowledge, all the evildoers who eat up my people as they eat bread and do not call upon the LORD? (Psalm 14:1-4)

We were also once foolish. Even those raised in a Bible-believing church have not always understood salvation or stayed the course. Many Christians stray from the path for a time. Some have even continued in one sin or another after finding faith. Riding the fence is not acceptable.

For we ourselves were once foolish, disobedient, led astray, slaves to various passions and pleasures, passing our days in malice and envy, hated by others and hating one another. (Titus 3:3)

If we have been continuing in sin or feeling in our heart God's Holy Spirit telling us that we need to change a specific behavior, we should listen. We cannot lie to ourselves, and we cannot lie to God. We cannot fool God. He sees, and He knows if we are planning to continue in our sin. Living for Christ means being honest with ourselves and with Him.

Living for Christ is not popular. As Christians, we will not be well-liked in the world. The world will label us as crazy, foolish, and gullible. But we are not any of the things non-believers call us. We are wise in the Holy Spirit. We know the truth, and we know that living a genuine Christian life will make a difference to those around us.

A 41-year-old felon accepted Christ in his heart while in prison. The change in him was remarkable. He was indeed a new creation. He went from an angry, violent gang member to a loving follower of Christ who lived what he believed. He trusted the Lord to be by his side and to guide him.

In prison and when he was released, he spent a year

loving those around him, volunteering to help others, attending church, and taking care of his family. He was in a great deal of physical pain due to a hernia, other health issues, and his 500-pound weight, but that did not stop him. He spoke to others and told them what Christ had done for him.

After a year on the outside, a car accident killed him. Many were devastated by his loss. Even a corrections officer cried when he heard the news. Men from prison wrote letters saying how he had impacted them for Christ. Our lives for Christ matter, no matter how long or how short.

You adulterous people! Do you not know that friendship with the world is enmity with God? Therefore whoever wishes to be a friend of the world makes himself an enemy of God. (James 4:4)

Our lives are a testimony that is seen by all. It shows that we have truly become new and are born again in Christ. The world is not our friend. Once Christ has washed us clean of our past, we live to show others His love and the difference that life with Christ can make.

As Christians, we know that God will bless us and will never leave us. We will not be shaken. We will not be overcome. We will find joy even in times of sadness. Living for Christ is the only way to have the peace and contentment we look seek.

I bless the Lord who gives me counsel; in the night also my heart instructs me. I have set the Lord always before me; because he is at my right hand, I shall not be shaken. Therefore my heart is glad, and my whole being rejoices; my flesh also dwells secure. (Psalm 16:7-9)

11

MATURITY

We know that living for Christ, though rewarding, can be difficult. Long-time Christians often become complacent or self-satisfied. Those who have been Christians for a short while can get drawn off into diverse topics and issues that remove them from the basics of salvation. New Christians are just trying to live their new life and learn all they can.

Our Christian lives encounter the world and the evil in it, and they are trying to destroy what God has given us. Of course, we genuinely desire to live for Christ, but the struggle to do so is real.

And no wonder, for even Satan disguises himself as an angel of light. (2 Corinthians 11:14)

Be sober-minded; be watchful. Your adversary the devil prowls around like a roaring lion, seeking someone to devour. (1 Peter 5:8)

We raise our children and try to help them mature, teaching and guiding them as they grow in knowledge, logic, and reasoning. We want them to become solid and good people. God is the same with us, His children. He wants us to mature in our knowledge and relationship with Him.

But grow in the grace and knowledge of our Lord and Savior Jesus Christ. To him be the glory both now and to the day of eternity. Amen. (2 Peter 3:18)

When we accept Christ, believing in God the Father, God the Son, and God the Holy Spirit, we are, as Christ said, "born again." We start as babes in Christ. Like human children, we need to be guided and taught to mature and grow in grace and knowledge of our Lord.

God does not want us to remain babies forever. Young Christians may easily be led astray by the lies of the world. They may listen to the false teaching that is deceitful but sounds good. The devil is cunning, and he knows what we want to hear. We must grow up by learning from God's Word and from those in the body of Christ who speak the truth.

So that we may no longer be children, tossed to and fro by the waves and carried about by every wind of doctrine, by human cunning, by craftiness in deceitful schemes. Rather, speaking the truth in love, we are to grow up in every way into him who is the head, into Christ, from whom the whole body, joined and held together by every joint with which it is equipped, when each part is working properly, makes the body grow so that it builds itself up in love. (Ephesians 4:14-16)

Christians must fact-check what we hear or learn about Christ and how He wants us to live against His Holy Word. He will never add to or take away from what He has taught us. The Holy Spirit helps us with this. We can pray for guidance. We can mature as Christians by allowing the Holy Spirit to speak to our hearts. Walking hand in hand with God every step and learning and practicing God's word is how we can grow.

Therefore let us leave the elementary doctrine of Christ and go on to maturity, not laying again a foundation of repentance from dead works and of faith toward God... (Hebrews 6:1)

Becoming a Christian, being born again is only the

beginning of our journey to maturity. Repentance of sin is constant because we continue to sin but accepting the gift of salvation through the foundation of repentance is not something we must repeatedly do. ("not laying again a foundation of repentance..." it says in Hebrews).

This scripture means that though we should admit when we sin, God knows our hearts and that we are repentant even if we do not verbally repent daily. We do not have to accept Christ into our hearts repeatedly either. He loves us and forgives us, and knows what we are doing, and He wants us to come to Him with our sins, our worries, our joy, our worship, and everything in our lives.

We can lose our salvation by turning our backs on God and continuing in a life of sin. In that instance, we would need to come back to Him, ask for forgiveness, and express our genuine belief in Him. His word says that in the last days, some will fall away. Some will depart from the faith, but we must be strong in our faith. The time of His return is near.

The blood of Christ has covered us. We have accepted Him as our Lord and Savior. Now it is time to grow in grace and knowledge and go on to maturity. Now is not the time to say, "I'm saved, and that's all I need."

Now the Spirit expressly says that in later times some will depart from the faith by devoting themselves to deceitful spirits and teachings of demons... (1 Timothy 4:1)

Now that we have come to know the truth of God our Creator, His Son's birth and death for our sins, and His resurrection, we have a relationship with Christ and should speak with Him often. We try to live for Him by reading His Word and listening to the teachings of those He has called to teach. And yet, we must be careful that what we are hearing or reading (even this book) is in line with His Word. God will never contradict Himself.

Therefore we must pay much closer attention to what we have heard, lest we drift away from it. (Hebrews 2:1)

There will be many who try to confuse us. There will be some who teach a different doctrine, like the student who wanted to convince me that God is a woman. These days can seem scary, but we are not afraid because God is with us. The most beautiful part of being a Christian is our confidence that He never leaves us, even for a moment. We never need to fear what is happening around us. We have peace. We have what everyone wants.

Christ lives in us by His Holy Spirit. The closer our relationship with Him, the more our hearts will tell us when something is not correct. With maturity comes discernment. God has and will continue to write His will on our hearts. Listen.

Take care, brothers, lest there be in any of you an evil, unbelieving heart, leading you to fall away from the living God. (Hebrews 3:12)

I have been crucified with Christ. It is no longer I who live, but Christ who lives in me. And the life I now live in the flesh I live by faith in the Son of God, who loved me and gave himself for me. (Galatians 2:20)

"As this world spirals down into hell, we need the Holy Spirit to help us stand strong by becoming mature followers of Christ. If we remain babies, we continue in immature thinking and will always be frustrated wondering why life isn't what we expected.[5]

For though by this time you ought to be teachers, you need someone to teach you again the basic

---

5   "For Thine Is the Kingdom and the Power and Glory Forever." Lord Teach Us to Live: Lessons on Daily Living from the Lord's Prayer, by JENNIFER CHAMBERLAIN, DOVE CHRISTIAN Publishers, 2020, pp. 170–170.

principles of the oracles of God. You need milk, not solid food, for everyone who lives on milk is unskilled in the word of righteousness, since he is a child. But solid food is for the mature, for those who have their powers of discernment trained by constant practice to distinguish good from evil. (Hebrews 5:12-14)

Satan is also real, and he is the enemy of God, trying to destroy everything God loves. He will try to keep us focused on our struggles and the world's problems so that we lose our peace and cannot reach others for Christ. If he cannot steal our salvation, he will steal our joy and maturity, making us fearful, ignorant, and unable to do anything for God.

...until we all attain to the unity of the faith and of the knowledge of the Son of God, to mature manhood, to the measure of the stature of the fullness of Christ... (Ephesians 4:13)

12

GOD'S WORD BRINGS UNITY, NOT DIVISION

The Bible is God's inspired word and is valuable beyond measure to us as Christians and those who want to understand Christianity. The information in the Bible may be too complex for us to understand, and much of this information does not affect our salvation. Still, it can affect our maturity and the abundant life that Christ wants us to live.

The Bible is highly profitable to us while we try to navigate this sinful world, and we should study God's Word diligently. God wrote every word, using human writers through the inspiration of the Holy Spirit, and the Holy Spirit will help us understand His meaning.

All Scripture is breathed out by God and profitable for teaching, for reproof, for correction, and for training in righteousness, that the man of God may be competent, equipped for every good work. (2 Timothy 3:16-17)

God's word teaches us how to live and how to react to the world. His Word tells us when we have done wrong and corrects us, putting us back on the right path. His Word trains us in the ways of Christ so we can go out and spread this simple Christianity with others. The Bible does this with stories, history, parables, laws, suggestions, and prophecies.

God's Word is both literal and not literal. Just as Jesus often spoke in parables to illustrate His point, there are stories in both the Old and New Testaments from which we can learn that may or may not be literal. If God felt it was important enough to include, then we need to read and study it, whatever it may be.

Some prophecies were proven true over time, such as Christ's birth, death, and resurrection. There are historical facts about kings and wars, of which we have records separate from the Bible.

Instructions that were true at the time of the writing, under the law of Moses, may not be applicable for today. Even the words of Christ, such as 'plucking out your eye if it causes you to sin,' are not literal, BUT there is always a lesson.

> *"The graphic word pictures of Matthew 5 and 18 still grab attention today, and they raise the question of how literally we should take Jesus' commands in these passages. Does Jesus actually mean to say that we should pluck out our eyes or sever a hand if we are prone to sin? It may be of comfort to know that Jesus' instructions in these particular verses are not meant to be taken literally. We need not mutilate our bodies as a punishment for our sin. Rather, Jesus means that we should be prepared to make exceptional sacrifices if we want to follow Him (see Matthew 16:24)."[6]*

And if your eye causes you to sin, tear it out and throw it away. It is better for you to enter life with one eye than with two eyes to be thrown into the hell of fire. (Matthew 18:9)

Recognize the point of this scripture from Matthew. We don't tear an eye out and throw it away, but what about a friend who is leading us into sin? We may need to remove them gently from our lives. Family members,

---
[6] GotQuestions.org

too, if they are sinning and taking us with them. These types of scripture hold valuable lessons for us. We must think them through, asking God for knowledge and wisdom.

Some events or facts were written so that the people of that day could understand them. Today's understanding is much different, not better or worse, but if we think about what it was like living during that age, we might better understand why things were written the way they were.

People who lived during various times when the Bible was written practiced an oral tradition. The people passed stories on by telling them to each generation verbally. This is not to imply that these stories are wrong or became confused in the telling because God's Holy Spirit breathed these stories to the tellers. However, through the writers, God described His miraculous works in terms that would be understood by the people of that time.

Stories were not written down until many years after each event. For instance, the book of Genesis, the world's creation, is believed to have been written by Moses between 250-400 years later. That seems like a long time to us, but 400 years after the creation of the universe is not that long, especially when humans were living anywhere from 120 years to 969 years, according to Wikipedia. The passing of the recollections of Adam and Eve may have only passed two or three generations.

Their language, traditions, and lifestyles were not like ours or even like those in the time of Christ. The Holy Spirit teaches us to think seriously and logically when reading God's Word for added perspective on the context of the writing.

Much of the history of wars, prophecies, and rulers are recorded elsewhere and can be verified. Therefore, we know that we have both literal and non-literal parts of the Bible. None of this information, except what concerns God the Father, God the Son (Christ and His resurrection), and God, the Holy Spirit, is required for our salvation, but all of the Bible is precious for us to read because it is all God's word.

Your word is a lamp to my feet and a light to my path. (Psalm 119:105)

In God's Word, He explains why He did things the way He did. Throughout the entire Bible, His love for us shines through, and He outlines His plan to bring us into a genuine and close relationship with Him.

Studying the Bible is as vital for our souls as food for our bodies. Unfortunately, choosing one topic from the Bible to analyze to the point of obsession and basing theology on it can cause individuals and groups to become involved in divisive discussions and arguments that lead away from the fundamental truths of salvation.

For example, Genesis states that God created the heavens and the earth in six days and rested on the seventh. We do not know, nor do we need to know for sure, whether it was six literal days, six thousand years, or six million years. Some will try to tell us that we must believe that creation happened in six literal days. Thinking the story is literal is fine, but having questions about it has no effect on our salvation and should not lead to a lack of unity among believers.

In the beginning, God created the heavens and the earth. The earth was without form and void, and darkness was over the face of the deep. And the Spirit of God was hovering over the face of the waters. And God said, "Let there be light," and there was light. And God saw that the light was good. And God separated the light from the darkness. God called the light Day, and the darkness he called Night. And there was evening

and there was morning, the first day. And God said, "Let there be an expanse in the midst of the waters, and let it separate the waters from the waters." And God made the expanse and separated the waters that were under the expanse from the waters that were above the expanse. And it was so. And God called the expanse Heaven. And there was evening and there was morning, the second day. And God said, "Let the waters under the heavens be gathered together into one place, and let the dry land appear." And it was so. God called the dry land Earth, and the waters that were gathered together he called Seas. And God saw that it was good. And God said, "Let the earth sprout vegetation, plants yielding seed, and fruit trees bearing fruit in which is their seed, each according to its kind, on the earth." And it was so. The earth brought forth vegetation, plants yielding seed according to their own kinds, and trees bearing fruit in which is their seed, each according to its kind. And God saw that it was good. And there was evening and there was morning, the third day. And God said, "Let there be lights in the expanse of the heavens to separate the day from the night. And let them be for signs and for seasons, and for days and years, and let them be lights in the expanse of the heavens to give light upon the earth." And it was so. And God made the two great lights—the greater light to rule the day and the lesser light to rule the night—and the stars. And God set them in the expanse of the heavens to give light on the earth, to rule over the day and over the night, and to separate the light from the darkness. And God saw that it was good. And there was evening and there was morning, the fourth day. And God said, "Let the waters swarm with swarms of living creatures, and let birds fly above the earth across the expanse of the heavens." So God created the great sea creatures and every living creature that moves, with which the waters swarm, according to their kinds, and every winged bird according to its kind. And God saw that it was good. And God blessed them, saying, "Be fruitful and multiply and fill the waters in the seas, and let birds multiply on the earth." And there was evening and there was morning, the fifth day. And God said, "Let the earth bring forth living creatures according to their kinds—livestock and creeping things and beasts of the earth according to their kinds." And it was so. And God made the beasts of the earth according to their kinds and the livestock according to their kinds, and everything that creeps on the ground according to its kind. And God saw that it was good. Then God said, "Let us make man in our image, after our likeness. And let them have dominion over the fish of the sea and over the birds of the heavens and over the livestock and over all the earth and over every creeping thing that creeps on the earth." So God created man in his own image, in the image of God he created him; male and female he created them. And God blessed them. And God said to them, "Be fruitful and multiply and fill the earth and subdue it, and have dominion over the fish of the sea and over the birds of the heavens and over every living thing that moves on the earth." And God said, "Behold, I have given you every plant yielding seed that is on the face of all the earth, and every tree with seed in its fruit. You shall have them for food. And to every beast of the earth and to every bird of the heavens and to everything that creeps on the earth, everything

that has the breath of life, I have given every green plant for food." And it was so. And God saw everything that he had made, and behold, it was very good. And there was evening and there was morning, the sixth day. (Genesis 1:1-31)

Whether or not God created the universe in six days, His word still teaches us that on the seventh day, He rested. Later, the law of Moses given by God to the people of Israel required that they rest on the Sabbath or seventh day, which they did. God wanted humankind to have a day of rest. God's word is so extraordinary that, literal or not, there is always a message for us today if we will only see it. The Holy Spirit will show us what is true.

"The international standard ISO 8601 counts Sunday as the seventh and last day of the week. However, Sunday is considered the first day of the week in many countries, including the United States, Canada, and Japan.

Sunday is a working day in most Muslim countries and in Israel." [7]

The Sabbath or seventh day of the week is Saturday in some cultures and Sunday in others, but many churches in the United States worship on Sunday.

*"Jewish communities around the world have since the Diaspora kept track of the **seventh** day **Sabbath;** and all agree it is the day commonly known as **Saturday**."* [8]

We have already established that we are no longer under the law of Moses since Christ's death and resurrection. We are now under the covenant of grace (not law). Therefore, many churches choose to worship on Sunday, not because they think it is the Sabbath (al-

---

7 https://www.timeanddate.com/calendar/days/sunday
8 www.avoiceinthewilderness.org www.avitw.ca

though some do), but because they believe Sunday to be the day Christ rose from the dead. These churches celebrate the resurrection every Sunday by holding services on that day.

There is a great deal of discussion about whether Saturday or Sunday is the first day of the week and is genuinely the seventh day. Is this what we should be spending our time on? Whatever day we fellowship with other believers is our choice under the grace of Christ.

It is good to dedicate a day of rest to the Lord and fellowship, though our salvation does not depend on it. Early believers often met on the first day of the week. Again, having questions about this does not affect our salvation and should not lead to a lack of unity among believers.

On the first day of the week, when we were gathered together to break bread, Paul talked with them, intending to depart on the next day, and he prolonged his speech until midnight. (Acts 20:7)

Can I be blunt? Don't fight over this or any other issue that has no bearing on salvation.

We can get so embroiled in a discussion about a part of the Bible or a particular scripture that it completely takes over our lives and beliefs. We can get so stuck on one thing that our relationships with God and others suffer. It is good to study the Bible but not get so wrapped up in one topic in the Bible that we base our salvation on it or get into arguments about it. Unity comes from loving each other as Christ loves us and refusing to get entangled in conversations that cause discord.

When I was in college, about four of us decided to study the casting out of demons. We were 19 years old and oh, so wise in our own minds. One young man got so involved with people who thought a demon-possessed them that he spent evenings late into the night praying and trying to cast out the demons. His schoolwork and his relationship with God suffered because that was all that was on his mind.

I realized after a while that even though I was not a regular participant, my relationship with God was suffering because I was neglecting Him and thinking more about the devil. I remember very clearly scolding myself and thinking that I must get back to the basics of salvation. I have recalled that moment many times over my 62 years.

God's word also discusses what we can eat or drink, which differed from the Old Testament to the New. Science shows that God's laws concerning food in the Old Testament saved the people from diseases and death. As sanitation, refrigeration, and cooking progressed, and we were no longer under the law, God began to show that eating some of those things was acceptable.

And he became hungry and wanted something to eat, but while they were preparing it, he fell into a trance and saw the heavens opened and something like a great sheet descending, being let down by its four corners upon the earth. In it were all kinds of animals and reptiles and birds of the air. And there came a voice to him: "Rise, Peter; kill and eat." But Peter said, "By no means, Lord; for I have never eaten anything that is common or unclean." And the voice came to him again a second time, "What God has made clean, do not call common." This happened three times, and the thing was taken up at once to heaven. (Acts 10:10-16)

God always takes care of His children and what we eat has no bearing on our salvation.

God's word covers everything we need to know and shows us what He wants us to do. The food we choose to eat and drink is between God and us, but He wants us to consider something. God's word instructs us how to behave with other Christians who might be bothered by what we do.

As Christians, we must always contemplate what effect our actions will have on other believers, new and old, and their faith. If we decide to eat meat, knowing that it bothers the person we are with, or choose to have an alcoholic drink with Christians who think it is a sin, we may cause them to question our faith or their own. We do not want our actions to force others to stumble. We should not want others to follow our behavior and end up with guilt and regrets because they believe it is a sin in their hearts.

But whoever has doubts is condemned if he eats, because the eating is not from faith. For whatever does not proceed from faith is sin. (Romans 14:23)

It is good not to eat meat or drink wine or do anything that causes your brother to stumble. (Romans 14:21)

Our choices affect those around us. God's word is so remarkable that it addresses all situations. It is not for us to judge others for their choices or convince them we are right. We are to think of other's welfare in the faith and their salvation before we think of our comfort or wants.

Do nothing from rivalry or conceit, but in humility count others more significant than yourselves. Let each of you look not only to his own interests, but also to the interests of others. (Philippians 2:3-4)

We would do well to read God's word daily. Everything we need to know is in there. With today's technology, we can google "what does the Bible say about_____?" and find a multitude of scripture and other writings about various subjects and life challenges (Remember to consider the context).

We can become so twisted up about specific areas of discussion that we neglect to spend time with God, strengthening our relationship with Him and admitting our failings. We forget what the absolute essentials are for our salvation, which is when we have a problem.

Discussing and researching various subjects in the Bible is fascinating and can be rewarding. If these discussions lead to disagreements and disunity or make us angry and judgmental towards others, we are not right in our relationship with God. We may even become self-righteous, thinking we have all the answers.

Paul wrote the following to Timothy, and we should all write these words on the first page of our Bibles.

O Timothy, guard the deposit entrusted to you. Avoid the irreverent babble and contradictions of what is falsely called "knowledge" (1 Timothy 6:20).

And in his second letter, he writes this:

Remind them of these things and charge them before God not to quarrel about words, which does no good, but only ruins the hearers. (2 Timothy 2:14)

Our sincere and pure devotion to Christ and His teaching is what is valuable for our lives. Humankind has struggled since Adam and Eve lost their close relationship with God. But Christ has redeemed us, so we can again have that closeness. It is up to us to show love and unity among the followers of Christ, even when we disagree about parts of God's Word that have no bearing on our salvation. The world is watching.

The Holy Spirit will lead us in discerning the Word. He will teach us to be humble when we speak about it. God's word is GOD, the Creator of the Universe, Father,

King, the great I AM, and though He shows us through His Holy Spirit many truths, we are still ignorant children and can easily be led astray.

> **But I am afraid that as the serpent deceived Eve by his cunning, your thoughts will be led astray from a sincere and pure devotion to Christ. (2 Corinthians 11:3)**

> **We know that we are from God, and the whole world lies in the power of the evil one. (1 John 5:19)**

The world lies in the power of the evil one who fell from grace and is the enemy of God. This situation will not always be. Christ will return, and our enemy will be defeated. We live in the world but are not part of the world. We are Christ's, and we must focus on Him crucified for the redemption of our sins and His resurrection.

> **If you were of the world, the world would love you as its own; but because you are not of the world, but I chose you out of the world, therefore the world hates you. (John 15:19)**

Satan can use research, opinion, and debating of scripture to mess with our minds and draw us away from the simplicity of Christianity. We reason that what we are doing is honorable because we are studying the Bible, after all. But he will use every trick, every subject, every media report, every Facebook argument, every virus, and every political event to fill our minds with anxiety, fear, anger, evil, and even hatred of others. We must guard our hearts and minds against these tricks by reading God's great word and allowing the Holy Spirit to teach us.

The world does not know the truth because it does not know God's word and does not know God. Therefore, the world bombards our minds with all kinds of negative thoughts and feelings. We must fight the battle for our minds daily, but we will only win if we allow God to fight it with us.

The Holy Spirit's discernment of God's word is what will win the fight. It is a battle for our very souls. We can only navigate this evil by reading about and living our lives after Christ's example, with love.

Finally, brothers, whatever is true, whatever is honorable, whatever is just, whatever is pure, whatever is lovely, whatever is commendable, if there is any excellence, if there is anything worthy of praise, think about these things. (Philippians 4:8)

We will find Christians focusing solely on individual scriptures written in letters to particular groups of people and basing theology on them. We will need to ask the Holy Spirit to reveal the truth and study the context of these scriptures. Even other Christians will mention trivial ideologies, which have valuable information and lessons but could also stir up strife among the body. Be aware.

Study scriptural subjects, but do not let them take away or add to what is necessary for salvation. Christ's burden is not heavy, and when we start focusing on these matters to the exclusion of pure faith in Christ, we put a burden on ourselves and other believers, just as Paul spoke about in his letter to Galatia.

Paul had preached the simple, absolute message of salvation through Christ and not through the law or rules made by man. Paul taught that we are justified through our faith in Christ and nothing else. He taught love and unity and that we are to believe, repent, and strive to live as Christ lived.

Study to shew thyself approved unto God, a workman that needeth not to be ashamed, rightly dividing the word of truth. (2 Timothy 2:15 KJV)

13

TITHING

"A tithe is a one-tenth part of something, paid as a contribution to a religious organization or compulsory tax to government. Today, tithes are normally voluntary and paid in cash or cheques, whereas historically tithes were required and paid in kind, such as agricultural produce." [9]

Giving a portion of our income to God can seem like a burden. When bills are high, and money is low, kids need clothes and school supplies, or the car breaks down, giving 10 percent of what is already not enough is hard to do.

Some churches and denominations make tithing compulsory and may even teach that not giving is a sin. Every week when the plate passes to you, you may feel stressed or guilty. But this is not what God wants you to feel.

"Jesus had more to say about money than he did about heaven and hell combined! In fact, the only subject Jesus talked about more than money is the Kingdom of God! And some of his teaching on the Kingdom of God dealt with money too.

"Therefore, money is critically important. Our atti-

---

[9] "Tithe." Wikipedia, Wikimedia Foundation, 7 Aug. 2021, en.wikipedia.org/wiki/Tithe.

tude towards money and how we manage it is the foundation that sets the stage for every other aspect of our spiritual lives. And if our understanding of money lays the foundation of our spiritual lives, then tithing is the place we need to start."[10]

Each one must give as he has decided in his heart, not reluctantly or under compulsion, for God loves a cheerful giver. (2 Corinthians 9:7)

If money and how we manage it are a foundational teaching for our spiritual lives, we had better pay attention. God's Word teaches us all we need to know about every subject, and money is no exception. God wants what is best for us, and He knows that if we allow our finances to get out of control, we will not have peace. Therefore, setting aside a portion for God is a lesson in being responsible.

2 Corinthians says that we must give as we have decided in our hearts. This statement is part of the new covenant of grace through Christ. What is necessary is that we stick to what we have promised.

Under the law of Moses, the people were commanded by God to set aside a tenth of their yield. Again, there are scriptures, some from the Old Testament, about what they were to give and why.

Bring the full tithe into the storehouse, that there may be food in my house. And thereby put me to the test, says the Lord of hosts, if I will not open the windows of heaven for you and pour down for you a blessing until there is no more need. (Malachi 3:10)

One of the promises of God is that when His people are faithful in tithing, God pours down blessings

---

10   Cree, Chris and Lisa. "2 Ways God Promises to Benefit You for Tithing." NewCREEations, 9 May 2016, newcreeations.org/god-promises-benefits-tithing/.

on them. He wants us to keep our word. He also wants us to be responsible for what we have. The tithes make us faithful, feed other people in need, and are a form of worship to God.

At the end of every three years you shall bring out all the tithe of your produce in the same year and lay it up within your towns. And the Levite, because he has no portion or inheritance with you, and the sojourner, the fatherless, and the widow, who are within your towns, shall come and eat and be filled, that the Lord your God may bless you in all the work of your hands that you do. (Deuteronomy 14:28-29)

Every tithe of the land, whether of the seed of the land or of the fruit of the trees, is the Lord's; it is holy to the Lord. (Leviticus 27:30)

We can all understand that sometimes it is difficult to give that full tenth, but we wonder how God feels when that happens. Will choosing to withhold some of our income from God stop us from going to heaven? No. But we may miss out on some of His blessings.

If we have promised to give a tenth faithfully and don't keep our promise, that does not please God, and we have not learned the lesson that He wants us to understand. So if we feel that we cannot give for a time in our lives or only give a portion, we need to tell Him. Talk it over with God. He will lead you one way or another. We must follow His leading. We have His promise to provide for us in all situations.

Give, and it will be given to you. Good measure, pressed down, shaken together, running over, will be put into your lap. For with the measure you use it will be measured back to you." (Luke 6:38)

The point is this: whoever sows sparingly will also reap sparingly, and whoever sows bountifully will also reap bountifully. (2 Corinthians 9:6)

Salvation does not depend on tithing, but God has told us that 1) we are to give; 2) we will be blessed if we give; 3) we honor Him when we give; 4) we show responsibility when we give willingly; 5) we support His church: 6) we help others when we give, and 7) we will reap bountifully. Faithfulness in our promise to Him is the key, not the amount given.

We forget that we can talk to God our Father just like we talk to anyone. We can tell Him about our expenses and our fear of not having enough. We can even make payment arrangements with our Father. Give 5 percent for three months or whatever you can; be faithful to what you promise and be responsible with your funds. If we tell God we can't give and buy things we don't need, there is a problem. We cannot lie to God nor mock Him.

Sell your possessions and give to the needy. Provide yourselves with moneybags that do not grow old, with a treasure in the heavens that does not fail, where no thief approaches and no moth destroys. For where your treasure is, there will your heart be also. (Luke 12:33-34)

It is more important to God that we be honest and faithful in our worship, including giving some of what we have. By being faithful to God, we show Him where our heart truly lies. We make it clear that He is more important than our wants or desires on earth.

When we give as we are able, it is vital not to make a show of it. We are not to be proud or think we are special because we give to the Lord.

Beware of practicing your righteousness before other people in order to be seen by them, for then you will have no reward from your Father who is in heaven. "Thus, when you give to the needy, sound no trumpet before you, as the hypocrites do in the synagogues and in the

streets, that they may be praised by others. Truly, I say to you, they have received their reward. But when you give to the needy, do not let your left hand know what your right hand is doing, so that your giving may be in secret. And your Father who sees in secret will reward you. (Matthew 6:1-4)

When issues like tithing come up, all we need to do is talk to Him. He will bless us for coming to Him with an open heart and a willingness to do what He asks of us. Everything God does or asks of us is for our benefit.

If God has blessed us to be rich in this world, we are no better than anyone else and should use our blessings to bless others.

As for the rich in this present age, charge them not to be haughty, nor to set their hopes on the uncertainty of riches, but on God, who richly provides us with everything to enjoy. They are to do good, to be rich in good works, to be generous and ready to share, thus storing up treasure for themselves as a good foundation for the future, so that they may take hold of that which is truly life. (1 Timothy 6:17-19)

We can all be rich in good works. We can all give of our time and our talents for the Lord. If money is not available for you to share, give something else. Be generous and trust God to meet your needs. Watch for what He does because it will be so unexpectedly different from what you think He will do.

It is not the amount you give that matters to God; it is your heart as you sacrifice that He sees.

And he sat down opposite the treasury and watched the people putting money into the offering box. Many rich people put in large sums. And a poor widow came and put in two small copper coins, which make a penny. And he

called his disciples to him and said to them, "Truly, I say to you, this poor widow has put in more than all those who are contributing to the offering box. For they all contributed out of their abundance, but she out of her poverty has put in everything she had, all she had to live on." (Mark 12:41-44)

The poor widow had great faith that God would meet her needs. She did not give a tenth; she gave 100 percent. There are many ways we can give to God. Yes, the church needs money to function and to bring others into the body of Christ, but God does not need our money. He needs our faithfulness and our trust.

Do not neglect to do good and to share what you have, for such sacrifices are pleasing to God. (Hebrews 13:16)

You shall give to him freely, and your heart shall not be grudging when you give to him, because for this the Lord **your God will bless you in all your work and in all that you undertake. (Deuteronomy 15:10)**

Whatever you decide that you can give, give without hesitation, without doubt, and worry. God loves us and is never hateful. He will not hold a grudge. This truth is hard for some of us to understand because the people around us are not this way. God is. Relax in His love and care. He knows your heart.

14

WATER BAPTISM

Many topics come up in Christian conversation and teaching that can cause confusion or division, more than this book can hold. Still, I would like to address water baptism and the debate among Christians about whether it should be by immersion into water or if sprinkling water is acceptable. As always, this is between you and God, but here are a few thoughts.

Some denominations add water baptism to the essentials for salvation. God does indeed ask that we be baptized. Christ himself was baptized by John the Baptist at the start of His ministry. He directed the disciples to baptize those who believed in Him.

Go therefore and make disciples of all nations, baptizing them in the name of the Father and of the Son and of the Holy Spirit... (Matthew 28:19)

To think our loving Father would turn away from someone who was either baptized by the sprinkling of water or unable to be baptized at all is unthinkable. If you feel that you must be baptized one way or another, it is the right thing to do for you.

Here is one of those subjects that can cause division among members of the body of Christ. It is a discussion that can draw us away from Him because of the disagreements of His followers. Baptism is essential; that is clear. Whether they brought in a big tub of water like we do in some churches or whether they used what they had available (the river) is not clear.

Can anyone withhold water for baptizing these people, who have received the Holy Spirit just as we have? (Acts 10:47)

We know that baptism was done chiefly by submersion in water, usually a river or stream, in the lives of John the Baptist and the early believers. Much of this is recorded in the New Testament. But we can see in Acts 10:47 that water was not withheld. This is said in such a way that we could presume that water was brought in from somewhere. Others have studied this more, but I try to stay within the bounds of my knowledge, and what I know for sure is that we should all be baptized because Christ said so. I do not believe it is crucial to our salvation.

Is water baptism symbolic as in washing our old selves away, or was this to show our death to self and resurrection with Christ? There are scriptures about both washing away our sins and dying and resurrecting as Christ did.

Having been buried with him in baptism, in which you were also raised with him through faith in the powerful working of God, who raised him from the dead. And you, who were dead in your trespasses and the uncircumcision of your flesh, God made alive together with him, having forgiven us all our trespasses... (Colossians 2:12-13)

And Peter said to them, "Repent and be baptized every one of you in the name of Jesus Christ for the forgiveness of your sins, and you will receive the gift of the Holy Spirit. (Acts 2:38)

Could it be that immersion was just because there were rivers and lakes around, and it was convenient? I do not know, but this is an issue that can become an uncomfortable burden for some. When discussing this subject, let us always err on the side of grace, accepting that God will deal with the heart of the person whose baptism we are questioning. Salvation comes through faith in Christ. The water does not save us.

John also was baptizing at Aenon near Salim, because water was plentiful there, and people were coming and being baptized (John 3:23).

Recently, a local prisoner wanted to be baptized but preferred to wait until he was out of prison to share the experience with his family. Unfortunately, he passed away while in prison. Do we believe for one minute that our loving God would not accept him? By no means! I do not think anyone who truly knows God could imagine such a thing. Baptism is important because it is what Christ asks of us, and it is a way we show the world our commitment to Him, but He sees what is in our hearts, and that is what is most important.

For as many of you as were baptized into Christ have put on Christ. (Galatians 3:27)

"When used in the New Testament, this word more often refers to our union and identification with Christ than to our water baptism. e.g. Mark 16:16. 'He that believes and is baptized shall be saved'. Christ is saying that mere intellectual assent is not enough. There must be a union with him, a real change, like the vegetable to the pickle!" [11]

The real change comes when we believe, repent, and live our lives for Christ.

Being sprinkled as a child or baptized as a baby is not a genuine commitment to follow Christ because the child is not at an age where they can decide for themselves. However, once a person reaches a proper under-

---

11   Boice, James Montgomery. Bible Study Magazine, May 1989.

standing of what Christ has done for them, has repented of their sin, and desires to live for Him, they can seek the baptism in whatever way God leads.

> **What shall we say then? Are we to continue in sin that grace may abound? By no means! How can we who died to sin still live in it? Do you not know that all of us who have been baptized into Christ Jesus were baptized into his death? We were buried therefore with him by baptism into death, in order that, just as Christ was raised from the dead by the glory of the Father, we too might walk in newness of life. For if we have been united with him in a death like his, we shall certainly be united with him in a resurrection like his. (Romans 6:1-5)**

We would not want to put undue pressure on someone sprinkled by making them think they are not saved because they have not been immersed in water. Each of us wants to show the world and God that we have entirely dedicated ourselves to Him and that we want a personal relationship. We are changed from the inside out, and we want the world to know. That is what baptism is all about.

15

THE HOLY SPIRIT

The issue of the Holy Spirit can also cause some division in the body of Christ. We know from God's word that we have the Holy Spirit when we accept Christ as our Savior, just as when He breathed on the disciples and said "receive the Holy Spirit" before the day of Pentecost.

> **When he had said this, he showed them his hands and his side. Then the disciples were glad when they saw the Lord. Jesus said to them again, "Peace be with you. As the Father has sent me, even so I am sending you." And when he had said this, he breathed on them and said to them, "Receive the Holy Spirit." (John 20: 20-21)**

But God's word speaks of the Holy Spirit as a helper in two ways. The first I will cover is a second baptism called the baptism in the Holy Spirit with the sign or evidence to the believer of speaking in other tongues in prayer. Jesus said the Holy Spirit is with us and that the Holy Spirit would also be in us, and He told the disciples to wait for that baptism in the upper room at Pentecost. Jesus promised to send His Holy Spirit to us as a helper after He ascended to the Father.

> **And while staying with them he ordered them not to depart from Jerusalem, but to wait for the promise of the Father, which, he said, "you heard from me; for John baptized with water, but**

> you will be baptized with the Holy Spirit not many days from now." (Acts 1:4-5)
>
> When the day of Pentecost arrived, they were all together in one place. And suddenly there came from heaven a sound like a mighty rushing wind, and it filled the entire house where they were sitting. And divided tongues as of fire appeared to them and rested on each one of them. And they were all filled with the Holy Spirit and began to speak in other tongues as the Spirit gave them utterance. (Acts 2:1-4)

There are many thoughts on the baptism of the Holy Spirit. Some believe that the evidence of speaking in tongues was just for that time and place, has drifted away, and is not for us now, but Peter said the promise was for all who were far off and to everyone whom the Lord calls to Himself. Did he mean distance, or did he intend it to mean far off in time?

> Now when they heard this they were cut to the heart, and said to Peter and the rest of the apostles, "Brothers, what shall we do?" And Peter said to them, "Repent and be baptized every one of you in the name of Jesus Christ for the forgiveness of your sins, and you will receive the gift of the Holy Spirit. For the promise is for you and for your children and for all who are far off, everyone whom the Lord our God calls to himself." And with many other words he bore witness and continued to exhort them, saying, "Save yourselves from this crooked generation." So those who received his word were baptized, and there were added that day about three thousand souls. (Acts 2:37-41)

Some believe that the evidence of speaking in tongues is still available (it seems arrogant of us to decide whether or not God can still provide this baptism) but not important enough to preach about and only causes problems and divisions in the church.

Some Christians believe the <u>baptism of the Holy Spirit</u> with the evidence of speaking tongues is the same as the **gift** <u>of tongues and interpretation for the church</u>. The initial baptism of the Holy Spirit, to which speaking in tongues is given as proof, is different than the **gift** of tongues and interpretation, which is one gift among other gifts from the Holy Spirit for the church.

1 Corinthians talks of the gifts given to and for use in the church. They are not the same as the baptism of the Holy Spirit. We have the Baptism (1), and we have the Gifts (2). Not everyone who is baptized with the Holy Spirit will be given the gift of tongues and interpretation for the church.

Here is a reference to the **gifts** of the Holy Spirit for the church.

To another the working of miracles, to another prophecy, to another the ability to distinguish between spirits, to another various kinds of tongues, to another the interpretation of tongues. (1 Corinthians 12:10)

Now back to the baptism. Some Christians believe that this baptism in the Holy Spirit is a second work of grace (the first being salvation) available to anyone who asks for it, even today. Therefore, many Pentecostal churches encourage those who come to Christ to seek this baptism and pray in tongues privately.

It is my belief (and you must decide for yourself) that when we accept Christ, we have the Holy Spirit breathed on us as Christ did with the disciples, but that we can ask for the second work of grace, the baptism in the Holy Spirit with the evidence of speaking in tongues in our prayers.

(Though this book is for your information and for you to make your own decisions as led by the Holy Spirit, I feel I must tell you of the excellent understanding, clarity of God's word, and boldness that the Holy Spirit has giv-

en me since I received this baptism with the evidence of speaking in tongues. It has opened my ears and heart to hear from God in a most amazing way.)

If we look at the earliest believers, we find that accepting Christ, being baptized in water, and sometimes even before being baptized in water, the believers were baptized with the Holy Spirit, which manifested itself by the believer speaking in other tongues.

The baptism of the Holy Spirit with the evidence of speaking in tongues is either mentioned straight out or inferred in many scriptures. A few are listed here.

> **While Peter was still saying these things, the Holy Spirit fell on all who heard the word. And the believers from among the circumcised who had come with Peter were amazed, because the gift of the Holy Spirit was poured out even on the Gentiles. For they were hearing them speaking in tongues and extolling God. Then Peter declared, "Can anyone withhold water for baptizing these people, who have received the Holy Spirit just as we have?" And he commanded them to be baptized in the name of Jesus Christ. Then they asked him to remain for some days. (Acts 10:44-48)**

> **Now when the apostles at Jerusalem heard that Samaria had received the word of God, they sent to them Peter and John, who came down and prayed for them that they might receive the Holy Spirit, for he had not yet fallen on any of them, but they had only been baptized in the name of the Lord Jesus. Then they laid their hands on them and they received the Holy Spirit. (Acts 8:14-17)**

> **And it happened that while Apollos was at Corinth, Paul passed through the inland country and came to Ephesus. There he found some**

disciples. And he said to them, "Did you receive the Holy Spirit when you believed?" And they said, "No, we have not even heard that there is a Holy Spirit." And he said, "Into what then were you baptized?" They said, "Into John's baptism." ⁴ And Paul said, "John baptized with the baptism of repentance, telling the people to believe in the one who was to come after him, that is, Jesus." On hearing this, they were baptized in the name of the Lord Jesus. And when Paul had laid his hands on them, the Holy Spirit came on them, and they began speaking in tongues and prophesying. There were about twelve men in all. (Acts 19:1-7)

Likewise the Spirit helps us in our weakness. For we do not know what to pray for as we ought, but the Spirit himself intercedes for us with groanings too deep for words. And he who searches hearts knows what is the mind of the Spirit, because the Spirit intercedes for the saints according to the will of God. (Romans 8:26-27)

But you, beloved, building yourselves up in your most holy faith and praying in the Holy Spirit... (Jude 1:20)

As I began to speak, the Holy Spirit fell on them just as on us at the beginning. (Acts 11:15)

In writings other than the Bible, those baptized in the Holy Spirit with the evidence of speaking in other tongues are also mentioned.

Evidence of Speaking in Tongues in the Early Church

Chrysostom, Bishop of Constantinople, writes:

"Whoever was baptised in apostolic days, he straightway spoke with tongues, for since on their coming over from idols, without any clear knowl-

edge or training in the Scriptures, they at once received the Spirit, not that they saw the Spirit, for He is invisible, but God's grace bestowed some <u>sensible proof</u> of His energy, and one straightway spoke in the Persian language, another in the Roman, another in the Indian, another in some other tongues, and this made manifest to them that were without that it was the Spirit in the very person speaking. Wherefore the apostle calls it the manifestation of the Spirit which is given to <u>every man to profit withal</u>."

A.D. 400: Augustine, Bishop of Hippo, one of the four great fathers of the Latin Church and considered the greatest of them all:

"We still do what the apostles did when they laid hands on the Samaritans and called down the Holy Spirit on them in the laying-on of hands. It is expected that converts should speak with new tongues."

Paul and others often wrote about the baptism and the gifts of the Holy Spirit. Though some of what was said may not be understood by us, speaking in tongues was evident to the early believers and accepted as commonplace. They understood the baptism of the Holy Spirit and the evidence that showed the world that they had received this great gift by speaking in tongues when they prayed. They did not question it or decide they did not want it. The baptism and the gift were not just emotional feelings but actual manifestations of the Holy Spirit, as shown by speaking in tongues.

This baptism, what some call 'being filled with the Spirit' (a somewhat misleading phrase), is a private welcoming of the Holy Spirit within us that gives us great strength, boldness, and wisdom. From experience, when I received this baptism, the Bible (I was reading King James at the time) became so much clearer and easier to read. I was 19 years old, and the difference was noticeable. I was also filled with a boldness to share Christ with others. Today I continue to pray and sing in tongues as I feel led. It brings great joy and significantly eases my anxiety when I do not know how to pray. It is a private thing, never loud or for others to hear.

Now we will move on to the **gifts** provided by the Holy Spirit to edify the church body—the same Holy Spirit but for an entirely different purpose. Many scriptures that confuse us refer to the gift of tongues and how a person should use it in church, and that interpretation should always follow. This gift is for the church, not for the individual.

> **Now there are varieties of gifts, but the same Spirit; and there are varieties of service, but the same Lord; and there are varieties of activities, but it is the same God who empowers them all in everyone. To each is given the manifestation of the Spirit for the common good. For to one is given through the Spirit the utterance of wisdom, and to another the utterance of knowledge according to the same Spirit, to another faith by the same Spirit, to another gifts of healing by the one Spirit, to another the working of miracles, to another prophecy, to another the ability to distinguish between spirits, to another various kinds of tongues, to another the interpretation of tongues. All these are empowered by one and the same Spirit, who apportions to each one individually as he wills. (1 Corinthians 12:4-11)**

Those who have received the initial baptism of the Holy Spirit can seek these gifts. God wants to give us the spiritual gifts we need so that we can be encouraged as His children, serving, having great faith, healing, and changing the world for Him.

1 Corinthians speaks at great length about tongues and the other **gifts** intended to build up the body of believers (for the church), and this is where some of the confusion comes in. The Holy Spirit's use of tongues

discussed here is <u>not the same as the baptism of the Holy Spirit</u>, which is for private prayer. The gift is given for use in the church.

Pursue love, and earnestly desire the spiritual gifts, especially that you may prophesy. (1 Corinthians 14:1)

Do all possess gifts of healing? Do all speak with tongues [gift]? Do all interpret? (1 Corinthians 12:30)

If I speak in the tongues [gift] of men and of angels, but have not love, I am a noisy gong or a clanging cymbal. And if I have prophetic powers, and understand all mysteries and all knowledge, and if I have all faith, so as to remove mountains, but have not love, I am nothing. ... (1 Corinthians 13:1-2)

Loving each other and loving God is more important than these gifts for the church. If we love our neighbors as we love ourselves, we will succeed in helping everyone to draw closer to God. The gift of tongues and interpretation for the church, without love, is worthless.

So, my brothers, earnestly desire to prophesy, and do not forbid speaking in tongues. (1 Corinthians 14:39)

Simply put, there are tongues as evidence of a second <u>baptism</u>, a baptism in the Holy Spirit that privately gives us more boldness, knowledge, and wisdom and helps us to pray.

There is also the <u>gift</u> of tongues for the church, which should always be followed by interpretation for the church to benefit from the message. This two-part gift is to build us up in the family of God.

These are not necessary for salvation, but from the depth of my heart, I encourage everyone to seek the baptism of the Holy Spirit just as the early believers did.

16

DISCERNING TRUTH

Words of wisdom from the apostles, the prophets, and all of the teaching in the Bible are essential for us so that we can understand salvation and live in unity with each other and the rest of humankind who do not believe in God. However, we must look at the context of the writing. Who was writing, who was being written to, and what was going on at that time? The answers to these questions teach us what these writings mean.

For example, Paul's first letter to the Corinthians is full of instruction for the new believers as they worship together. First, he congratulated them on following the traditions he taught them and then discussed who the church and the family are.

This section of scripture can cause division if we do not look at the context of Paul's writing.

Now I commend you because you remember me in everything and maintain the traditions even as I delivered them to you. But I want you to understand that the head of every man is Christ, the head of a wife is her husband, and the head of Christ is God. (1 Corinthians 11:3)

From **Bible Notes Commentary,** we read that these verses are about Godly authority in the church and indicate that some of the women were usurping the male authority.

In those days, males always held leadership roles, so Paul spells out the correct order of church leadership for the Corinthians. First is God, then the male, then the female. For unity, every group of individuals must have one head, even today, but male or female leadership is acceptable today in the church. This change does not imply domination or dictatorship. Neither man nor woman can survive without the other.

It was also important for women to cover their heads and men to uncover their heads. I do not know why that was important, for as I have said, I am not a scholar on such matters, but for the church of Corinth to be in unity, Paul felt obliged to address this issue. We need to see what we can learn from it for our lives today.

Every man who prays or prophesies with his head covered dishonors his head, but every wife who prays or prophesies with her head uncovered dishonors her head, since it is the same as if her head were shaven. For if a wife will not cover her head, then she should cut her hair short. But since it is disgraceful for a wife to cut off her hair or shave her head, let her cover her head. For a man ought not to cover his head, since he is the image and glory of God, but woman is the glory of man. For man was not made from woman, but woman from man. Neither was man created for woman, but woman for man. That is why a wife ought to have a symbol of authority on her head, because of the angels. Nevertheless, in the Lord woman is not independent of man nor man of woman; for as woman was made from man, so man is now born of woman. And all things are from God. Judge for yourselves: is it proper for a wife to pray to God with her head uncovered? Does not nature itself teach you that if a man wears long hair it is a disgrace for him, but if a woman has long

hair, it is her glory? For her hair is given to her for a covering. If anyone is inclined to be contentious, we have no such practice, nor do the churches of God. (1 Corinthians 11:4-16)

I know of church theology built solely around women's long hair.

Paul's letter intended to instruct them to show the respect and honor of proper behavior in that period of history. They were to demonstrate to outsiders that they were in unity. When there are problems in the church, outsiders will see it, and we will lose our ability to show them the way. These issues of leadership were causing contention among some of the members in Corinth.

Men's hair was short, Paul says, because of nature. What was it in nature that caused men to have short hair? In the Old Testament, men would make an oath to God and allow their hair to grow long. Traditions of each age were important, but unity was and is always central in the body of Christ.

All the days of his vow of separation, no razor shall touch his head. Until the time is completed for which he separates himself to the Lord, he shall be holy. He shall let the locks of hair of his head grow long. (Numbers 6:5)

Following Christ's death and resurrection, Paul wrote to people living by grace and not the law, but this was unfamiliar territory for everyone. Women were coming to Christ just as men were. Some of the new believers were Gentiles who had not been following the law of Moses and did not follow those traditions. Jewish Christians still attended the Temple along with meeting together with the Apostles and other teachers. It was a confusing time for all, but the apostles wanted the believers to get along and have unity and to reflect the character of Christ. Logical thinking was applied to each situation, as it should be today.

Another issue was modesty, spoken of in 1 Timothy and 1 Peter, and the submission of wives to their husbands in Ephesians. These matters cause a lot of tension among some believers today.

Likewise also that women should adorn themselves in respectable apparel, with modesty and self-control, not with braided hair and gold or pearls or costly attire, but with what is proper for women who profess godliness—with good works. (1 Timothy 2:9-10)

As Christians, we know that we should not be showy, sexy, or out of control, but we are to live a life like that of Christ. We strive to be like Him in all things. But today, we have the same tendencies as the women in 1 Timothy and 1 Peter. The world is fixated on looks, clothing, jewelry, makeup, and outrageous acts of both men and women. Christian women and men need to be moderate, modest, and to show the love of Christ in a way that draws attention to Him and not to us. Still, this has no bearing on our salvation. Believe, repent, and live as Christ directs. He sees your heart.

Do not let your adorning be external—the braiding of hair and the putting on of gold jewelry, or the clothing you wear— (1 Peter 3:3)

Let your moderation be known unto all men. The Lord is at hand; (Philippians 4:5 KJV)

We must respect and honor each other. These days both men and women hold leadership positions in the church because this is not a sign of disrespect and does not or should not cause contention. We are all to be submissive to each other and show respect to Christ as the head of all. Love and unity are vital.

The topic of women in submission to their husbands is a scripture with which many struggle. Paul's letter to the Ephesians brings this out. Marriage was and still is regarded as the perfect union of body, mind, and spirit between a man and a woman. But the church in Paul's time was dealing with a world that was becoming very immoral, as it is today, and marriage was not being respected, even in the church.

In this passage, Paul is setting forth an ideal that shone with a radiant purity in an immoral world.[12]

Wives, submit to your own husbands, as to the Lord. For the husband is the head of the wife even as Christ is the head of the church, his body, and is himself its Savior. Now as the church submits to Christ, so also wives should submit in everything to their husbands. Husbands, love your wives, as Christ loved the church and gave himself up for her, that he might sanctify her, having cleansed her by the washing of water with the word... (Ephesians 5:22-26)

These Bible verses instructing women to submit to their husbands do not mean that women are not equal to men in God's sight. Women are equal children of God, given gifts from God, led into ministry, have wisdom, and many other wonderful traits that complement men's strengths. Even in the time of Paul, women were conducting Bible studies and holding meetings in their homes.

Many women in the New Testament taught the Good News to others. Women were and are today called of God to be ministers of the Gospel just as men are.

"The Bible's word for 'Submit' is hupakouó: <u>to listen, attend to</u> Original Word: ὑπακούω Part of Speech: Verb Transliteration: hupakouó Phonetic Spelling: (hoop-ak-oo'-o) Definition: <u>to listen, attend to</u> [13]

"We can see in Strong's definition that when women

---

12 Barclay, William. The Letters to the Galatians and Ephesians. Revised Edition ed., The Westminster Press, 1976.
13 Strong's Concordance

are told to be submissive to their husbands, they are being told to listen to them and attend to their ideas and opinions. This is not a matter of who gets the remote control. It's all about God's will." [14]

The word '**everything**' is also used when women are instructed to submit to their husbands. The Greek word in the Bible is 'Pas,' which means **all** in the sense of <u>each part that applies</u>. Looking at the writings to the church, we can, with logic and common sense, assume that Pas is related to the church and therefore concerning spiritual matters as the <u>'each part that applies.'</u>

> *pás ("each, every") means <u>"all" in the sense of "each (every) part that applies."</u> The emphasis of the total picture then is on "one piece at a time." (ananeóō) then focuses on the part(s) making up the whole – viewing the whole in terms of the individual parts.*

The apostle's letters written to the churches concern church matters. Unfortunately, we often take one sentence out of a letter in scripture and base our requirements for the behavior of a large portion of society on that one sentence. Without a further study of scripture, this can add unnecessary burdens and take away the simplicity of Christianity. We cannot pull out only those scriptures that support our ideas and expect other people to live by our rules.

But I want you to understand that the head of every man is Christ, the head of a wife is her husband, and the head of Christ is God (1 Corinthians 11:3)

> *"As every organization has a head, God desires the man to be the head of the household as Christ is the head of the man. This does not mean that there will always be agreement between the husband and*

---

14 "Thy Will Be Done on Earth as It Is in Heaven." Lord Teach Us to Live: Lessons on Daily Living from the Lord's Prayer, by Jennifer Chamberlain, Dove Christian Publishers, 2020, pp. 92–93.

wife or that the wife must always be in an attitude of servitude. Someone must have the final word as long as that word agrees with God's word." [15]

The scripture about women in submission was difficult for me considering my upbringing by powerful women. But I have worked in many organizations, and the successful ones had a leader. In church, at work, and in the family, there must be only one head. If either the man or woman is prideful and tries to control the other, that is not of God.

"Each person in a marriage has different strengths, experiences, and knowledge that help the family unit when making decisions. Each should be listened to and attention given to their specific wisdom. In many instances, the wife will have the final say because of her expertise. This shows wisdom and leadership on the part of the husband." [16]

"We are all one in Christ. We are the church body submitting to and listening to Christ. His word is profitable to us. His word educates us and leads us into the right decisions. The words of husbands who prayerfully study God's word and use wisdom in their homes will profit the entire family." [17]

Unity among Christians is what God wants, and when we allow ourselves to move off into these topics to the point that they become contentious, there is no unity. We should not be so self-focused that how we think others should behave overrides the love we should have for them. Loving our neighbor as ourselves is the second greatest commandment.

And one of the scribes came up and heard them disputing with one another, and seeing that he answered them well, asked him, "Which

---

15   ibid, page 93
16   ibid, page 93
17   ibid, page 94

commandment is the most important of all?" Jesus answered, "The most important is, 'Hear, O Israel: The Lord our God, the Lord is one. And you shall love the Lord your God with all your heart and with all your soul and with all your mind and with all your strength.' The second is this: 'You shall love your neighbor as yourself.' There is no other commandment greater than these." (Mark 12:28-31)

17

OUR IDEAS

As human beings, we tend to come up with ideas that seem reasonable to us, and although we want to do what God wants us to do, our ideas can make the Christian life difficult. God did not want our lives to be wearisome, He wanted them to be peaceful, loving, and abundant, but we think we know better.

There is a way that seems right to a man, but its end is the way to death. (Proverbs 14:12)

Most people believe themselves to be highly intelligent and logical. But God's intelligence is so far beyond what we can understand, and His logic is foolishness to the world.

We take a sentence of scripture written to specific people at a particular time, making it the basis for salvation, worship, and life. Though inspired by the Holy Spirit to instruct us, these scriptures are examples of living as Christ lived, not words to be twisted to mean what we want them to mean.

Every way of a man is right in his own eyes, but the Lord weighs the heart. (Proverbs 21:2)

Indeed, individual scriptures can encourage, exhort, strengthen, and help us in our daily lives. I have listed numerous specific scriptures in this book without going into a great deal of context. These scriptures are not the basis for salvation but only for instruction. Acceptance of Christ, His death, resurrection, and repentance of our sins are the simple steps to salvation through Him.

We can puzzle together some fascinating theology if we rely on individual scriptures from various books and letters. Indeed, we can find unique scriptures that support our own ideas. But the Bible, each book and letter, needs to be taken as a whole for the true meaning. When taking the entire Bible and looking at the context of each writing, there is no contradiction to be found.

When we decide that our ideas about Christianity are how people should live, we run into trouble and disagreements. Peace can only come through living, acting, and reacting as Christ did and would. "What would Jesus do?" was a popular phrase for a while, and though simple, it is an effective way to look at and react to the events in our daily lives.

We need to walk in God's light, not in our ideas or perceived understandings. We do not want to be false prophets. Not many are called to be Bible scholars. God has not called many of us to become teachers of His Word. Our ideas are not God's ideas.

Staying the course by being grounded in simple Christianity will never let us down. The basics are the basics. They never change, and they never will change. God is the same yesterday, today, and forever. So study, think, pray, and discuss the scriptures, but always check your ideas by the basics of salvation and in the context of what was written.

I am sure we will get to heaven and find out we got many things wrong, but God is merciful. He only asks us to believe, repent, and live for Him. He loves us, and His Word teaches us how to do what is necessary for salvation. So, we simple people need to check and double-check our ideas with God's word before sharing them.

But if we walk in the light, as he is in the light,

we have fellowship with one another, and the blood of Jesus his Son cleanses us from all sin. (1 John 1:7)

Remember the simplicity of salvation. We believe, we repent, and we live for Christ. All other discussions and topics must be subjected to the discernment of the Holy Spirit. We receive **knowledge** in many ways, but the **wisdom** that we receive from God through His Holy Spirit tells us how to use that knowledge. Be kind, loving, and non-judgmental. In other words, be as Christ would be and as God asks of us.

He has told you, O man, what is good; and what does the Lord require of you but to do justice, and to love kindness, and to walk humbly with your God? (Micah 6:8)

18

CONCLUSION

We are all desperate for life to be easier. Living a smooth, carefree life and having peace would be such a blessing. We want to be happy and have love in our lives, friends, and something to do that makes us feel valuable. Minute by minute, we strive to find this peace that can only be found through Christ. We go after substitutes for the real thing.

We want love, but we substitute sex with anyone at any time. We want joy, but we go after temporary happiness through parties and money, trying to forget our troubles.

We want peace, but we escape stress through drugs and alcohol. We are not patient, and we are not kind or good to each other. The world is full of selfish, faithless, harsh people with no self-control, and yet, we can't figure out why we have no peace. All types of evil acts are acceptable in our societies. The world is lost, but non-Christians continue to ridicule those who have found what they are looking for.

No matter what we do or how hard we try to find peace, all of us still have problems; we do not have the easy life we want. We are angry at other drivers, at the government, at our boss, and our spouse or children. We are like hamsters on a wheel doing the same things repeatedly and getting the same results. Satan has blinded our minds to the truth.

What we need is salvation through Jesus Christ. We need saving, not only from an eternity without God, but also from the stress and evil of the world, ourselves, and the false substitutions that the world is selling to us. The only way to have peace now and forever is to know God and have a personal relationship with Him. And it is not difficult no matter what we believe or have been told.

For God did not send his Son into the world to condemn the world, but in order that the world might be saved through him. (John 3:17)

When we seek Jesus, we do not need society or theologians to add more burdens than we already deal with in this world. Christ does not need additions, amendments, and instructions added to the Christian walk in the name of Christianity. Satan, through man, has interfered enough! The world is self-centered, and Christians are confused. He may think he has won, but he is wrong. God wins, and we will not be overcome.

It is time for us to be clear about Christianity. We need the family of God, those who worship in Spirit and truth. We need straightforward Bible teaching, and we need discernment from the Holy Spirit to show us what is and is not necessary for our salvation. We need to get back to basics and enjoy the abundant life that Christ wants us to have.

Christians must stop getting caught up in things that have little importance. Christ meant it to be simple, and it is until we begin to meddle. Christianity is a gift to be accepted or rejected; not choosing to believe is a choice to reject God, but there is a way to salvation.

Believe in God and His Son, Jesus Christ. Believe that Christ was born of a virgin and was completely man and completely God. Believe that He died on the cross for our sins and rose from the dead and now lives eternally. Repent of your sins and strive to live as Christ taught. This is what saves us and gives us the certainty that we will live eternally with Him. Let God take care of the rest.

Once we are born again, we are children of God and are privileged to have all the promises of Him at work in our lives. We have the Holy Spirit and can have more of the Holy Spirit for the asking. We have God with us always, strengthening us, giving us peace, holding us, and teaching us. He is our Father and loves us unconditionally, just as we are.

And my God will supply every need of yours according to his riches in glory in Christ Jesus. (Philippians 4:19)

We have His Word, the scripture to teach us, help us develop our relationship with Christ and each other, supply our needs, and direct our paths. If we have burdens, we can ask for strength, peace, faith, and more from God.

The noise of the world is loud, but God is louder. The chaos of the world is scary, but God is stronger than anything. He will calm the waters. We will not drown. We will not be overcome.

For I know the plans I have for you, declares the Lord, plans for welfare and not for evil, to give you a future and a hope. (Jeremiah 29:11)

We must keep our eyes on the simplicity of Christ and allow God to fill us with His peace. The world will not understand this peace, but they will see it in us. We can show God to them through the peace that we have even during the struggles of life. The world is longing for this peace. They want it, and we are the only ones who can tell them where to find it.

When you pass through the waters, I will be with you; and through the rivers, they shall not overwhelm you; when you walk through fire you

shall not be burned, and the flame shall not consume you. (Isaiah 43:2)

Others may be utterly obsessed with their "learning" and "knowledge," but we must always come back to simple Christianity by believing, repenting, and living for Christ. In this way, we will have peace and unity with our fellow believers.

Christianity was not meant to be complicated, worrisome, burdensome, scary, or any of those negative terms. Instead, it is full of the fruit of the Holy Spirit, love, joy, peace, patience, kindness, goodness, faithfulness, gentleness, and self-control. It is not religion. It is a choice to believe in and follow the one true God and have a relationship with Him.

But the fruit if the Spirit is love, joy, peace, patience, kindness, goodness, faithfulness, gentleness, self-control; against such things there is no law. And those who belong to Christ Jesus have crucified the flesh with its passions and desires. If we live by the Spirit, let us also keep in step with the Spirit. Let us not become conceited, provoking one another, envying one another. (Galatians 5:22-26)

Christianity is not a church. It is a relationship with our Father God, His Son, and the Holy Spirit. It is a way of life lived together with the One who created us, loves us, and saves us. We can walk on the stormy water if we keep our eyes on Christ. Believe, Repent, and Live for Him.

For God so loved the world, that he gave his only Son, that whoever believes in him should not perish but have eternal life. For God did not send his Son into the world to condemn the world, but in order that the world might be saved through him. (John 3:16-17)

Other books by Jennifer Chamberlain
Fresh Fruit: Meditations on the Fruit of the Holy Spirit
Lord, Teach Us To Live

www.ingramcontent.com/pod-product-compliance
Lightning Source LLC
Chambersburg PA
CBHW030912080526
44589CB00010B/268